W9-BNO-410

11/25/08

Mongolia

JENNIFER L. HANSON

INTRODUCTION BY P. RICHARD BOHR

Facts On File, Inc.

Nations in Transition: Mongolia

Facts On File, Inc.
132 West 31st Street
New York NY 10001

Library of Congress Cataloging-in-Publication Data

Hanson, Jennifer.
    Mongolia/Jennifer Hanson.
        p. cm. — (Nations in transition)
    Includes bibliographical references and index.
    ISBN 0-8160-5221-2
    1. Mongolia—History. I. Title. II. Series.
    DS798.5.H36 2003
    951'.7—dc21   2003044903

Text design by Erika K. Arroyo
Cover design by Nora Wertz
Maps by Patricia Meschino © Facts On File

Printed in the United States of America

MP JT 10 9 8 7 6 5 4 3 2 1

This book is printed on acid-free paper.

CONTENTS

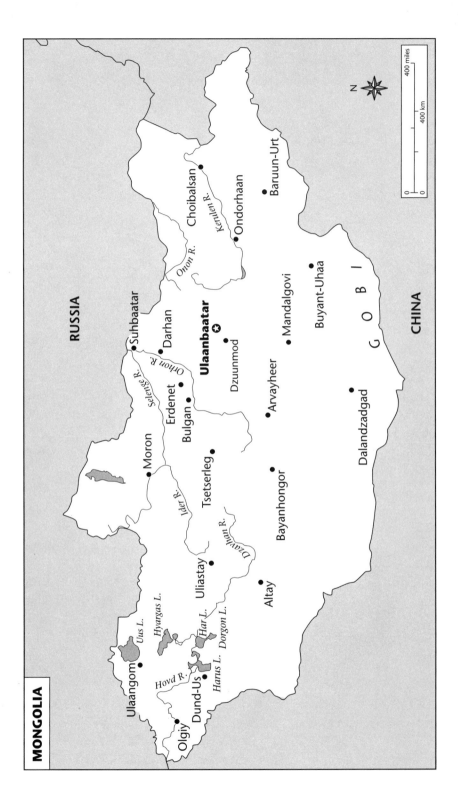

INTRODUCTION

Jennifer Hanson's lively book tells the remarkable story of Mongolia and its unique people. Best known for having once ruled history's largest land empire, the Mongols also created a vibrant culture, established Asia's oldest socialist republic, and—since their democratic revolution in 1990—are striving to transform their ancient nomadic society into a modern 21st-century nation.

Stretching along the vast Central Asian plateau 5,100 feet above sea level, Mongolia is twice as long as it is wide and is the world's largest land-locked country. Bordered by Russia to the north and China to the south, its terrain is diverse, stretching from alpine mountains and rolling hills to grassland sea and arid desert. Annually, Mongolia's northern half receives 10 inches of rainfall, while the south gets less than three inches.

With terrain too dry for permanent farming, the Mongolian steppe has been able to support enough grassland only for grazing animals to produce milk, meat, wool, and hides. Hence, the seasonal movement of herds from pasture to pasture became central to Mongol life and inspired a rich folk culture.

Descendants of the Huns of Central Asia, the Mongols organized themselves into shifting alliances along family, clan, and tribal lines. They worshiped shamanistic forces and minor spirits under Tengri, or "Eternal Heaven." They not only made their living from animal husbandry, but employed their horses to become the world's most fearsome mounted warriors, who often attacked cities and towns beyond the steppe.

In 1206, a number of Mongol tribes turned to Genghis (Chinggis) Khan (1162–1227), whom they proclaimed "universal sovereign," to unify them under his charismatic military and political leadership. Through an officer corps that included the sons of his own kinsmen and other clan and tribal leaders, Genghis created the world's finest cavalry. From boyhood, Mongol warriors were trained in the saddle. Carrying their food and dismounting only to change the animals conveying them, they could ride for 10 days at a stretch, covering as much as 270 miles per day. With iron discipline and tactical imagination, the mobile Mongol horse columns could encircle and decimate the enemy. Using a bow that could kill at 600 feet, the Mongols also employed psychological warfare, terror, and mass slaughter to demoralize their foes.

By the time Kublai Khan (1216–94), Genghis's grandson, came to power, a mere 1 million Mongols had knit together a diverse, polyglot Eurasian empire. Stretching from the Pacific Ocean to the Black Sea, the Mongols ruled Korea, Manchuria, China, northern Vietnam, Tibet, Turkistan, Afghanistan, Kashmir, Persia, Mesopotamia, Asia Minor, Russia, Poland, and Hungary. Only typhoons (*kamikaze*, or "divine wind") saved Japan from the invading Mongol ships. And only a succession struggle among the Mongol overlords spared western Europe from Mongol attack.

While the Mongols won their empire on horseback, they administered it through a law code, or *yasa*, supervised by educated civil servants who levied agricultural and commercial taxes on a far-flung, diverse population. During the century of *pax Mongolica*, the broad-minded Mongol rulers initiated a cosmopolitan age of East-West interchange. The Mongols patronized art and culture and promoted multiculturalism by exchanging Chinese, Turkish, Persian, and European artists, musicians, writers, astrologers, mathematicians, scientists, physicians, and others throughout their sprawling empire. While the Mongols adopted Tibetan Buddhism for themselves, they welcomed all religions, including Islam, Judaism, and Christianity. Kublai Khan himself invited Franciscan missionaries to build churches in Beijing and offer Gregorian chants in his palace.

Mongol rule also made possible Marco Polo's celebrated Asian travels, and it promoted prosperity by linking Asia and Europe through fortified trade routes for the exchange of furs, silks, porcelains, herbs, and mirrors, as well as the use of paper money. It also accelerated communications through a postal relay system in which mounted messengers could cover 200 miles a day. Over these roads, western Asia and Russia received many innovations from China: gunpowder, book printing, porcelain, textiles, medical discoveries, playing cards, and art motifs. In return, China was heavily influenced by the Arab and Turkish cultures.

Amid this impressive integration of far-flung peoples and cultures, strife among the Mongol rulers weakened imperial control. By the mid-14th century, the Ottoman Turks had pushed the Mongols out of western Asia. In the early 17th century, Inner Mongolia (within the Great Wall of China) was firmly under Chinese control, and by the end of that century, Outer Mongolia (outside the Great Wall of China) had become a Chinese province. Yet, in time, Outer Mongolia became a pawn in Asia's great-power rivalries. Both Russia and China held sway over it twice in the 20th century.

Ultimately, with the support of the Russian Red Army, Damdiny Süh-baatar (1894–1923), leader of the communist-inspired Mongolian Revolutionary Government, expelled the Chinese and anticommunist White Russians. On November 26, 1924, Sukhe Bator declared the creation of the Mongolian People's Republic (MPR), Asia's oldest people's republic. Determined to transform nomadic Mongolia into a secular, industrialized country like the Union of Soviet Socialist Republics (USSR), the MPR's closest ally and biggest patron, the Mongolian People's Republican Party monopolized political power. From it alone, candidates were recruited for election to the State Great People's Khural (Ikh Khural), the national assembly. In October 1961, the MPR was admitted to the United Nations.

The Mongol nomads were settled into cooperatives and collectives (organized labor groups) so that—in a country where animals outnumber humans by 25 to 1—central planners could develop an animal husbandry industry based on rendering; meat packing; and milk, cheese, wool, feather, and hide processing. Then, thanks to investments and expertise from other socialist countries, the MPR developed a heavy-industry sector that focused on coal, copper, gold, and molybdenum mining; oil refining; steel and cement production; carpet, shoe, and boot manufacturing; and railroad building.

Nevertheless, communism's challenges to the traditional Mongol lifestyle forced thousands of Mongols to seek refuge—with millions of heads of livestock—in Inner Mongolia during the Lama Rebellion of 1932. On the positive side, the urbanization accompanying industrialization resulted in a huge rise in literacy and the extension of needed health care. In addition, women soon came to make up half the country's workforce and gained prominence in professions such as law and medicine. In the aftermath of the demise of the Soviet Union and the fall of the Berlin Wall, political agitation in the MPR resulted in unprecedented multi-party elections and a new constitution mandating a democratic govern-ment and a progressively free-market economy. In 1996, Mongolia's Democratic Union Coalition formed the first noncommunist govern-ment in more than 70 years. Amids this new openness, the Mongols have returned to their rich, time-honored, Buddhist-inspired traditions. Free of communist constraints, they can now also celebrate the birthday of their national hero, Genghis Khan.

In the pages that follow, Hanson describes the return of Mongolia's traditions in colorful detail. She also discusses the daunting obstacles to Mongolia's economic development, including an inadequate financial, communications, and transportation infrastructure; a poorly trained workforce; and the country's remoteness from the global economy. There is growing tension between maintaining Mongolia's pastoral traditions and the price to be paid for economic development based on urban living and private property rights: a growing gap between rich and poor, gov-ernment corruption, domestic violence, homelessness, rising crime rates, environmental degradation, and persistent human rights abuses.

Wedding respected published scholarship with the most current Inter-net information to chronicle the Mongols' story, Hanson provides impor-tant insights into Mongolia's ability to integrate itself into a rapidly modernizing 21st-century Asia. However, the indispensable contribution of her book is her vivid portrayal of the buoyant Mongol spirit and deter-mination to succeed, which gives her readers a helpful framework in which to consider the prospects for Mongolia's future.

—P. Richard Bohr

PART I
History

1

THE RISE AND FALL OF THE MONGOL EMPIRE

Civilizations rise and fall at different times. When early humans were developing primitive tools in present-day Mongolia, North and South America were probably entirely uninhabited by people. When Greek and Roman culture flourished, Mongolian tribes were engaged in destructive border skirmishes with their Chinese neighbors. When Europe was languishing in the Dark Ages, Genghis Khan and his descendants were building, on horseback, the largest land empire the world has ever seen, promulgating a wise legal system, encouraging religious freedom, and living in splendor. It was not until recent centuries that East (Asia) and West (Europe and the Americas) met, with tumultuous consequences for Mongolia.

Prehistory

The land now called Mongolia has been inhabited for a long time. Evidence of human activity 500,000 years ago has been found in the country—axes made of river pebbles, sharp-pointed implements, disc-shaped flints. The people who used these were predecessors of the Neanderthal people. The climate of Mongolia was milder in this period than it is now. The mountains were covered with deciduous as well as coniferous forest.

Where the land is now dry, there were well-watered meadows frequented by antelopes, ostriches, Tartar foxes, and mammoths. Forty thousand to 50,000 years ago, the climate cooled, and glaciers grew and shaped valleys and depressions. Around this time, primitive Mongolians also developed finer tools—knives, spearheads, and scrapers for processing animal skins and wood. They also learned to make fire, build shelter, and wear clothing. In the late Paleolithic period—40,000 to 12,000 years ago—humans continued their intellectual development, to which cave paintings in Hovd province are a testament. The land was populated by large animals: remaining mammoths, hairy rhinoceroses, stags, bison, wild asses, and antelopes. In the Mesolithic period (12,000 to 7,000 years ago), primitive Mongolians began to use the bow and arrow (enabling hunting from a distance) as a weapon and to domesticate animals. They also began migrating—across a then-existing land bridge over what is now the Bering Straits—to North America.

Written descriptions of the Mongolians date back as far as 5000 B.C., courtesy of China, Mongolia's southern neighbor. They foretold the ensuing 7,000 years of history as well as describing the present. They suggest the mutual enmity, suspicion, and slander that has characterized the Mongolian-Chinese relationship at many times in their history. The accounts liken the Mongolians to wolves and barbarians, seeking to steal Chinese produce (China's land is much better suited to farming than Mongolia's). In later years, Mongolians would have reason to develop similar attitudes toward the Chinese encroaching on their land.

There is also evidence of improved agriculture and communal living from this period. Stone mortars and pestles that have been found demonstrate that Mongolians had grain that required processing—either grown wild or cultivated. Settled farming of grains and animals has historically represented evolution from hunter-gatherer societies. Findings of nephrite ware in Mongolia suggest that the people who crafted them must have begun trading by this time period, as the raw materials for making the nephrite ware were not available near the site where they were found.

From later eras, more physical evidence has survived. "Reindeer stones," granite monuments carved with images of stars, deer, tools, and weapons, have been discovered dating from 3000 B.C. or earlier. These survived—miraculously—above ground and unprotected from the elements, with drawings intact. Several hundred of them—some as tall as 15 feet—dot the Mongolian countryside. Partly from the images carved on the stones, we know that prior to 1500 B.C., the inhabitants of Mongolia both farmed and herded nomadically. Around that time and continuing afterward however, the climate grew even colder, making the growing season too short to farm crops well. Mongolians, therefore, still had reason to tame wild horses, yaks, and camels that could move easily in search of better pastures.

The period from about 2500 B.C. to about 1000 B.C. is conventionally known as the Bronze Age, and Mongolian ancestors' activities were true to the times. Mongolia is rich in copper deposits, which favored this metalwork (copper is the main ingredient in bronze). Household utensils and triple-bladed bronze pendants for women to wear as hair ornaments have survived. Some finds testify to the growing importance of domestic animals in Mongolian culture. Long daggers decorated with drawings of mountain goats and sheep have been discovered, as have red rock paintings of pens with dots indicating the animals inside. The art also shows animal and human figures standing hand in hand, and a spread-winged eagle presiding over the scene. Drawings of wheeled war chariots also provide evidence of horse breeding and wheeled transport in this era.

Although estimates vary, the Iron Age is thought of as beginning in 700–500 B.C. and lasting some 700 years. In Mongolia, iron instruments found date back to that time. Also dating to that period are "stone-cist" graves, in which the dead were laid on their back, sometimes with a stone pillow below their head, surrounded by their possessions. Excavations have unearthed mirrors, mouthpieces of bronze horse bits, earrings, bracelets, necklaces, axes, knives, plates, kettles, and striped red-and-brown earthenware vessels among these burial goods.

With improved weapons, craftsmanship, trading, and methods of herding, Mongolians were more capable of forming large clans and threatening their neighbors. The Xiongnu, a Mongolian tribe about which little is known, invaded China in the third century B.C. but was successfully repelled. In response, emperor Shi Huangdi of the Qin dynasty (221–206 B.C.) began building the Great Wall of China, enlarging and expanding previously built fortifications across northern China. Temporarily deterred, the Xiongnu turned their attention to a northwestern neighbor, the Yuezhi tribe, whom they eventually defeated after years of skirmishes. Once again, in the second century B.C., the Xiongnu attacked China, finding the 1,684-mile-long Great Wall not to be a serious obstacle. It was too long for the Chinese to adequately defend. The Xiongnu held much of China for a century or so, but were once again driven back into Mongolia. Other tribes gained and lost power, such as the Xianbei, the Toba, the Ruanruan, the Turk, conquering and then retreating from parts of China. The name *Mongol* to describe the northern enemies of the Chinese appears first to have been used during China's Tang dynasty (A.D. 618–907).

Genghis Khan

By the time of Genghis Khan, the tribes of Mongolia were ready for unification. They shared a similar language, appearance, culture, and ancestry. They even had common political goals, but each tribe on its own was no match for the powerful civilizations of Asia neighboring Mongolia. Under Genghis, they would get the revenge against past invaders, land, and access to lucrative trade routes they sought.

Having consolidated the tribes—an unprecedented accomplishment—Genghis began his conquest of the rest of Asia. He used both the forceful and the psychological techniques that had aided him in his rise among the Mongolians. First, he built a powerful army. Other than priests, undertakers, and doctors, all males aged 15 to 70 were required to join. In order to prevent squabbling among the various Mongol tribes, Genghis insisted that the cavalry units be made up of people from different tribes and promoted soldiers based on skill rather than tribal affiliation.

The organization of Genghis's military was superior to that of previous Mongol forces. Where soldiers in earlier Mongol armies had been jacks-of-all-trades, Genghis's soldiers were specialized. Some took care of horses, some organized the food supply, and some made strategic decisions. Genghis's soldiers were organized into units of 10, grouped into larger units of 100. Each 10-man and each 100-man unit selected its own commander. These smaller units were grouped into units of 1,000 and, eventually, 10,000. Genghis appointed the commanders of the larger units.

GENGHIS KHAN

The boy who became Genghis Khan (*Genghis* is an honorific title more recently transliterated as Chinggis) was born Temujin in approximately 1162. According to legend, he had a large ruby-like blood clot in his hand, a sign of future greatness, at birth.

Although his father was a prominent chieftain, Temujin's road to greatness was rocky. When he was about nine, his father went to find him a wife, a girl from a neighboring tribe. On his father's return home, he accepted hospitality from some men he encountered in the countryside, not recognizing them as people he had previously wronged. His hosts poisoned the food they offered him, and once he got home, he died. His tribe, the Kiyat, was now leaderless. One option for the Kiyat would have been to take Temujin as its new leader. Instead, the Kiyat abandoned Temujin, his mother, three brothers, two half brothers, a sister, and an old woman to live—and probably die—alone on the steppe (Mongolia's grassy plains). Surprisingly, the group survived, gathering berries, hunting birds and other small animals, and fishing (all untraditional ways for the herding Mongolians of getting food.) At a young age, Temujin showed himself willing to kill to survive and gain power. Accusing his older half brother of stealing a golden sparrow and a fish that Temujin thought were his to eat, he shot him dead with an arrow. This gave Temujin, now the oldest, a claim to leadership of the family.

Temujin continued his rise by forming alliances with other young men and, eventually, other clans of Mongolians. He showed generosity as well as violence in his rise, offering horses, food, furs, leadership, and beautiful women to those who joined him. By 1206, he was the acknowledged leader of all the Mongolians. He was given the name *Chinggis* [Genghis], meaning "great," or "oceanic," at a gathering of all of the tribes.

Genghis insisted on loyalty and unity within his army. He expected commanders to eat the same food as ordinary soldiers, and he looked for more than military skill in selecting them. In explaining why he rejected one potential commander, Genghis is reported to have said, "This man is indeed a hero and an able fighter. And it's true that he scoffs at hardship and ignores fatigue. But precisely because he assumes that every man who serves under him is like himself, he should not be in command of an army. A good commander . . . must understand what his followers feel—or he will allow his warriors to suffer and his horses to starve." Loyalty among the soldiers was expected as well. If part of a 10-man unit moved forward or retreated, the rest of the unit had to follow or be put to death. If one soldier was captured by the enemy, the rest of the unit had to rescue him or they would also be killed. Genghis knew that infighting and disorganization had prevented the Mongolians from conquering in the past, and he was determined to operate differently.

Genghis also developed a sophisticated support structure for his military, including a census to facilitate recruitment, a system of signal flags and flaming arrows to convey information on the battlefield, and a messenger system capable of connecting commanders across vast stretches of Asia. The system, which later functioned as Mongolia's postal system until 1949, was served by more than 100,000 horses, scores of postal stations, and a mandatory yearly service—for almost all herders—of 45 days.

Some of the messengers were riders, while others remained with their families and herds at a postal station. There, they put up a spare *ger* (traditional Mongolian tent) for riders and provided food for them. A rider might change horses five to six times a day, covering hundreds of miles in total. Marco Polo (1254–1324), the Italian trader who reported on Asia to Europe in the late 1200s, claimed that a letter could get from the Yellow Sea (between China and the Korean Peninsula) to the Adriatic Sea (east of most of Italy), the extent of the Mongol Empire, in a week.

Each shipment had a document attached to it so that the postal stations it passed through could stamp it with the name, date, and time of passage. Delays could result in fines or imprisonment. Rush deliveries were carried by special riders wearing gold or silver medallions with a falcon symbol. When these riders approached a station, they would blow a horn so that the postal workers would have a horse at the ready by the time they arrived. Envelopes containing rush deliveries also had a seal with bird and horse footprints, which meant to "ride at flying bird speed."

As for military training, Mongolians are trained from birth to ride horses and shoot bow and arrows (even today), so those skills required little work. Genghis needed to drill his army in military strategy, however, and he used three-month-long winter game hunts to do so. The tactics used to hunt animals served his armies well on the battlefield. One tactic, the feint, involves sending a few horseman forward to lure defenders out of their fortifications to fight a supposedly small army. The hidden attackers then emerge and seize on the vulnerable defenders. Another tactic, the "circle and close in," drives the enemy backward using a line of horsemen; eventually, the sides of the Mongol line close in to encircle the enemy.

Genghis's army conquered the Tangut people's empire of Xixia and the kingdom of the Jurchen, both in present-day northern China; Korea, which surrendered; and the rich Muslim kingdom of Khwarazm, in the region presently occupied by Kazakhstan, Uzbekistan, and Turkey. Genghis's rapacity became the stuff of legend. Writers at the time described massacres by his army of 1.6 million people at Herat, in present-day Afghanistan; 1.7 million at Nishapur, in present-day Iran; and 800,000 at Baghdad in Iraq. Sometimes Genghis was inclined to be merciful, relying on his reputation for violence to motivate enemies to simply surrender. For example, he sent diplomats to one kingdom hoping merely to begin trade relations. The governor of the kingdom chose to assassinate the diplomats—and paid for it dearly. When Genghis ransacked Bukhara, in present-day Uzbekistan, he is reported to have entered the chief mosque of the holy city and said, "I am God's punishment for your sins." By the time Genghis completed the conquest of Zhongdu (present-day Beijing, China), the streets were described as "greasy with human fat," the bones of the dead forming a giant white hill. Some have estimated that Genghis's armies slaughtered 30 percent of the population of Central Asia in the process of conquering it.

In the conquered regions, Genghis introduced improvements in civil (nonmilitary) society. Although his armies massacred populations, they spared artisans, architects, clerks, and other professionals who could be useful in running the empire. Genghis built a great capital at Karakorum, the site of present-day Kharkhorin/Horin in central Mongolia. The city was strategically located at the crossroads of trade routes. Its residents enjoyed religious freedom, and the city contained mosques and Christian churches as well as Buddhist temples. People from all over Asia were encouraged by the Mongols to take up residence in the capital.

The city was surrounded by protective walls and had four gates, one at each cardinal point. At each gate was a market. Grain was sold in the east, goats in the west, oxen and carts in the south, and horses in the north. *Gers* surrounded the city, outside the walls. As the city developed during Genghis's life and afterward, it grew more splendid. The Palace of Worldly Peace was the city's most impressive feature. Its floor tiles were heated from below. Its roof was covered in green and red tiles. A throne was covered in a panther skin. Elsewhere in the city, a French sculptor who had been captured by the Mongols in Hungary built an extraordinary fountain. It was in the shape of a silver tree, and it had silver lions' heads that dispensed mare's milk and golden snake heads that dispensed wine, rice wine, mead, and *airag*, the fermented mare's milk so popular among Mongolians. When a nobleman requested a drink, an angel atop the fountain held a bugle that could be blown to signal servants.

Genghis also developed a detailed legal code, or *yasa*. It incorporated traditional Mongol laws and also new ones appropriate to the extended Mongol empire. In addition to the usual prohibitions, such as against stealing, there were laws against lying and meddling in other people's quarrels, and laws requiring the return of lost property (in a herding society, people were not expected to keep tight control of their property in order to retain ownership of it). There were also laws against alcoholism, which Genghis saw as a threat to society and a waste of resources. Drinking was permitted, but if a man became drunk more than three times in a month he was punished.

Genghis also had laws that governed society as a whole. His military laws concerned relationships with other nations. He also established a safety net for Mongols who through tragedy or bad luck were unable to fully take care of themselves. He set up a fund to help the children of those killed in battle. If citizens were injured or disabled, Genghis made sure they had enough food and materials for basic survival. Genghis's generosity helped him maintain his leadership.

Genghis died in 1227 of injuries he received from falling off a horse. The Mongols who escorted his body back to the region of his birth killed every living thing they encountered—human and animal—so that they would be of use to Genghis in the next world. Tradition dictated that a ruler's burial place be kept secret, so the 2,000 people who attended Genghis's funeral were killed, as were the 800 soldiers who had executed them. Horses trampled the burial ground to disguise the digging marks. To this day, despite the best efforts of fortune-hunters looking for the treasures buried inside, Genghis's grave has not been found.

The Later Khans

A premonition of death had motivated Genghis to get his affairs in order. He divided his empire into four sections, or khanates, giving one to each of his four sons. Chagadai was awarded the southwestern part of the empire, or present-day Afghanistan, Turkistan, and central Siberia. Genghis's grandson Batu, inheriting through his father, Jochi, got control of central Eurasia and went on to establish the Golden Horde, which operated essentially independently of the rest of Mongolia. The Golden Horde eventually converted to Islam and allied itself with Russia. Tolui was given the homeland, central Mongolia. Ogodei, Genghis's favorite son, was given China and East Asia and succeeded to Genghis's paramount leadership position.

Ogodei reigned for 12 years, continuing the military push southeast to present-day Korea, further south in China, and westward, conquering present-day Russia, Ukraine, Poland, Lithuania, Hungary, and the Czech Republic. At the gates of Vienna, word came that Ogodei had died, and the armies were obliged by Genghis's law to return to Mongolia to elect a new great khan.

Mengke, grandson of Genghis and one of Tolui's sons, was elected khan. His armies resumed their activities in eastern Europe and pushed even further south in Asia, taking much of southern China and present-day northern Vietnam. While khan, Mengke rewrote the succession laws to limit the power of his cousins, Genghis's other grandsons. Mengke's brother Kublai (1216–94) succeeded him as khan in 1261.

Unlike his predecessor khans, Kublai showed interest in and talent at not only conquering lands, but also ruling them. Kublai established his winter court at Dadu (Zhongdu)—present-day Beijing, China. Though khan of Mongolia, Kublai was also the first emperor of the Yuan dynasty (1280–1368) of China. He fostered trade throughout the empire, encouraged scientific study, improved Chinese agriculture, and developed the Mongol script, which derives from the ancient Vighur (Turkic) script. Kublai attempted to expand the Mongol Empire across the sea by conquering Japan and Java (present-day Indonesia), but storms in the Sea of Japan repelled his forces twice and he did not succeed. The Mongols were horsemen, not seamen. Nonetheless, this was the height of the Mongol Empire.

PERSPECTIVE ON THE MONGOLIAN EMPIRE

Although the suffering inflicted by Genghis Khan and his successors upon their fellow Mongols and others was extreme, creating an orderly society out of a disorderly one almost always comes at a price. America, France, Colombia, Germany, and Italy, to name just a few, all fought wars for the sake of unification, and some of the most organized societies in the world like Saudi Arabia are run by absolute monarchies. Moreover, many of the khans were generous once they felt sure of their power, and in some areas were always progressive. Freedom of religion is a rather recent development in the West, but the Mongolian khans were practicing it 700 years ago. Women were treated far better in the Mongolian Empire than they are in much of the Middle East today or than they often were in the Victorian period in the West. Perhaps the tragedy of the Mongolian Empire is that many of its success in law, communications, art, and trade lasted such a short time in relation to the cost in human life they exacted to come into being. Perhaps we would consider the American Civil War to have been entirely tragic rather than almost glorious if the Union had dissolved five years after the North won.

It did not stay intact long. Some have compared the Mongolians to the Vikings, who terrorized the North Sea and reached America around the same time. The Mongols, too, had conquered through terror tactics and military prowess but lacked the numbers of people or the will to successfully administer their territory after Kublai Khan died. The Mongols were expelled from China by the Ming (1368–1644) in 1368.

As the Mongol Empire collapsed in China and South Asia, the structure Genghis and his heirs had imposed on the homeland of central Mongolia also broke down. Mongol society began to resemble the feudal order of Europe around the same time and earlier, with various local noblemen running their own territories uncontrolled by an overarching leader. This noble class was composed of former military leaders. The foot soldiers became herders much like the rest of the population.

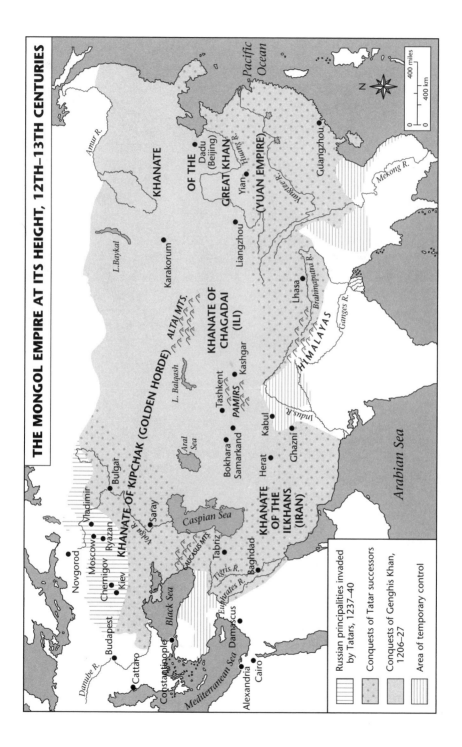

THE MONGOL EMPIRE AT ITS HEIGHT, 12TH–13TH CENTURIES

KHANATE OF THE GREAT KHAN (YUAN EMPIRE)

Dadu (Beijing)
Yian
Liangzhou
Karakorum
Guangzhou

Pacific Ocean

Amur R.
Huang R.
Yangtze R.
Mekong R.

KHANATE OF CHAGADAI (ILI)

L. Baykal
Lhasa
Brahmaputra R.
HIMALAYAS
Ganges R.
Kashgar

KHANATE OF KIPCHAK (GOLDEN HORDE)

ALTAI MTS.
L. Balqash
PAMIRS
Tashkent
Bokhara
Samarkand
Herat
Kabul
Ghazni

Indus R.

Aral Sea

KHANATE OF THE ILKHANS (IRAN)

Bulgar
Vladimir
Novgorod
Moscow
Ryazan
Chernigov
Kiev
Saray

Volga R.
Caspian Sea
CAUCASUS MTS.
Tabriz
Baghdad

Tigris R.
Euphrates R.

Budapest
Cattaro
Constantinople
Black Sea
Damascus
Cairo
Alexandria

Danube R.
Mediterranean Sea
Arabian Sea

Russian principalities invaded by Tatars, 1237–40
Conquests of Tatar successors
Conquests of Genghis Khan, 1206–27
Area of temporary control

N

400 miles
400 km

天同日昭

*Young men joined monasteries in such large numbers that Mongolia's popula-
tion was affected.* (Courtesy Library of Congress)

Life was not entirely peaceful and stagnant, however. Various groups
of Mongols continued to skirmish with the Chinese, causing China's
Ming emperors to reinforce the Great Wall. The two main Mongol tribes,
the Oirat and the Khalka, fought a lengthy civil war from 1400 to 1454.
The Oirat won. Later, in the next century, Altan Khan (1507–83) united
the Khalkas and defeated the Oirat.

Altan Khan's reign was also notable because it initiated the spread
of Buddhism in Mongolia. Kublai Khan had welcomed Buddhism into
the Mongol Empire, but as one among many religions citizens could
practice. Now, Tibetan Buddhism was adopted as the state religion,
becoming one of many factors that tamed the Mongols' appetite for
war-making in the following centuries (for more on Buddhism, see
chapter 7).

The other factors contributing to this change in lifestyle included the
leadership style and the military capabilities of Mongolia's new neighbor
to the South, the Qing dynasty of China. The Qing, Manchu invaders

from Manchuria in northeastern China, ruled from 1644 to 1911. One of the reasons they were able to wrest control away from the Chinese Ming dynasty was their superior firepower. They possessed very effective muskets and cannons, which were also effective against the Mongols. Mongols on horses with bows and arrows were no match for these weapons, and Mongol society was not adapted to produce or purchase such arms. Mongolia had a barter/subsistence economy, whereby families produced food and necessary items for themselves and conducted limited trade with others.

During the Qing dynasty, the breakdown of the old Mongol Empire became complete, and Mongolia's new, narrower boundaries more final. Northern Mongolia became subject to the Russian czar (emperor). Southern, or "Inner," Mongolia (so-called because it was on the southern, Chinese side of the Great Wall of China) officially became part of China, and remains so today. Even "Outer" Mongolia, the area farther from China that makes up present-day Mongolia, became subject to Chinese rule. Mongolia itself also became somewhat more settled. Buddhism

Chinese merchants controlled the Mongolian economy in the period before the communist revolution. (Courtesy Library of Congress)

encouraged the growth of fixed cities around lamaseries (Buddhist monasteries). Previously, the nomadic lifestyle of the Mongols had given rise to few urban centers.

The Revolution(s)

If in the course of centuries of Qing rule Mongolia seemed relatively peaceful, this was about to change. As the 20th century dawned, governments in both China and Russia were overthrown; Japan was rising militarily; and Mongolia once again became a battleground for warring powers.

The Qing dynasty of China, which had ruled for more than 250 years, fell in 1911 to the republican Nationalists led by Sun Yat-sen (Sun Yixian) (1866–1925). China's last imperial dynasty had ended. Mongolia seized the chance to declare itself independent of China, and there was little that the struggling China could do about it. Russia, eager to have Mongolia on its side, encouraged such "independence," while actually hoping to control Mongolia. It gave Mongolia money, weapons, ammunition, and other help in training its army. China finally accepted the situation, signing a treaty in 1915 that officially gave it control of Inner Mongolia while recognizing the independence of Outer Mongolia.

Soon, however, Russia as well became too distracted to protect Mongolia adequately. It became involved in World War I, and in 1917 also suffered a coup. The Russian czar was overthrown by the White Russians, a more moderate group supported by the West, who soon became embroiled in civil war with the communist Bolsheviks. Recognizing an opportunity, China moved into Mongolia again. Japan also moved into Mongolia, hoping thereby to gain an advantage over the Chinese and one of the warring factions within Russia. China prevailed, and Mongolia surrendered to the Chinese in 1919.

Once again, Russia responded. Although still battling the Bolsheviks, some White Russians were driven east, away from the centers of power in European Russia. Russian baron Roman Nikolaus Fyodirovich von Ungern-Sternberg, the "Mad Baron," driven out of Russia as much by his mental state as by his politics, was one of these. He decided that his mission would be to save Mongolia from the Chinese.

The Mad Baron believed that he was the reincarnation of Genghis Khan. Those who knew him described him as monsterlike in appearance, his eyes staring at people psychotically like those of an "animal in a cave." He had a sword scar on his forehead that bulged when he became upset, which apparently was often. The baron was attended by a friend nicknamed "Teapot," who strangled whomever the baron was with when the baron called for a teapot. Another adviser, Colonel Sepailov, had a mental and physical disorder that caused him to shake, talk, and drool constantly.

These figures might have been sympathetic if not for their barbarism. The baron's military tactics in some ways resembled that of Genghis, his supposed former self. The baron roasted deserters alive, baked prisoners of war, and also murdered people by throwing them into locomotive boilers.

Arriving in Mongolia in 1920, the baron accomplished his initial mission of liberating Mongolia from the Chinese. It was not a very difficult task, as the Chinese had not had to occupy Mongolia heavily in order to guarantee the cooperation of the populace. After expelling the Chinese, however, the baron pillaged Ulaanbaatar, a commercial center and later capital of Mongolia, and allowed his men to loot the Mongolian treasury. Soon after, he declared himself emperor of Russia, with no justification.

In an effort to stop the madness, two native Mongolian leaders, Sukhe Bator (1893–1923) and Khorloghiyin Choibalsan (1895–1952), asked the Communists, members of which party were now in control of Russia, for help. Russia (by now known as the Soviet Union) agreed and joined forces with Mongol troops led by Sukhe Bator to retake Mongolia. The allies succeeded, and Mongolia declared independence on July 11, 1921. Sukhe Bator became a national hero. The Soviets executed the Mad Baron later that fall. Soon after in 1923, Sukhe Bator died at a very young age. Some suspect the Soviets of having killed him, too, although the evidence is not complete.

Between 1921 and 1924, Mongolia's governmental system and international allegiances were in turmoil. The country officially was a limited monarchy. Jebtsundamba Khutuktu (1869–1924), a religious leader, called the living Buddha, who had led Mongolia during previous brief periods of independence, was named leader. Mongolia also had a

THE POWER OF BUDDHIST MONASTERIES

Although Mongolia was technically under the control of the Manchu dynasty of China through the beginning of the 20th century, such control bore some resemblance to that exercised by Britain upon the 13 American colonies. It was weak, exercised in large part from far away, somewhat corrupt, and left room for local leaders to wield power.

Much of that power was wielded by the Buddhist monasteries. The monasteries had grown in power through their relationship with Mongolian noble families. Many noble families sent children to become monks in order for them to escape military duty. They also claimed to have discovered reincarnations of religious leaders in their families, perpetuating their influence over the church. Reincarnation in increasingly higher spiritual forms is an important tenet of Buddhist theology, but is difficult to prove and so can be subject to manipulation. As late as the 1930s, the annual income of the Buddhist church was approximately equal to that of the Mongolian government. In the United States in 2002, by contrast, the income of the federal government was approximately 300 times larger than that of the largest religious group, the Catholic Church.

The monasteries, in fact, operated like the government, although many would say they performed their religious tasks much better than their governmental ones. They produced great art and religious texts, but their education system left most Mongolians illiterate and their health care system left room for communist improvement.

temporal leader, Premier Bodo. The leadership of both of these was short-lived. When Bodo sought to distance Mongolia from the Soviets, he and many associates were arrested, charged with counterrevolutionary activities, and executed. Jebtsundamba died in 1924, and the government prevented the traditional search for a reincarnation of the religious leader. Another would-be leader who wanted to resist Soviet influence was arrested and executed in the same year. On November 25, 1924, Mongolia adopted a Soviet-style constitution and officially became the People's Republic of Mongolia, a communist state, only the second in the world. China would not become communist until 1949, after World War II.

NOTES

pp. 7–8 "'This man is indeed a hero . . .'" Quoted in Miriam Greenblatt, Genghis Khan and the Mongol Empire (New York: Benchmark Books, 2002), pp. 17–18.

p. 8 "Marco Polo . . ." cited in "Urtuu, Medieval Post," in Mongolia Today, Issue 4. Available on-line. URL:http://www.mongoliatoday.com/issue/4/urtuu.html. Posted 1999–2002.

p. 9 "'I am God's . . .'" Quoted in Bradley Mayhew, Richard Plunkett, and Simon Richmond, Central Asia (Melbourne, Australia: Lonely Planet Publications Pty Ltd, 2000), p. 20.

p. 9 "greasy with human fat . . ." Quoted in Greenblatt, Genghis Khan and the Mongol Empire, p. 24.

p. 12 "Some have compared . . ." Guy Gugliotta, "The Mongol Mysteries: Are 'Deer Stones' a Clue?" in The Seattle Times, August 14, 2002. Available on-line. URL: http://seattletimes.nwsource.com/html/nationworld/134512886_nomads13.html.

p. 17 "'animal in a cave . . .'" Quoted in Bradley Mayhew, Mongolia (Melbourne, Australia: Lonely Planet Publications Pty Ltd, 2001), p. 22.

2

THE COMMUNIST ERA

Mongolians did not exactly choose communism and status as a Soviet satellite, but they did not exactly resist them, either. By now, perhaps, they were so accustomed to foreign troops and control of their affairs that one power's involvement did not seem terribly different from another's. In addition, the country was not centrally administered at this point, so Soviets overrunning the capital of Ulaanbaatar probably did not directly affect the life of a herding family making its way from pasture to pasture, at least not for a while. Due, among other factors, to internal Soviet politics, World War II, and the disorganized condition of Mongolia, communism took a long time to fully establish itself.

In addition to violence, the Soviet era was also characterized by an improved standard of living for Mongolians, better social services, the development of industries other than agriculture, and more contact with the outside world than Mongolia had had for many centuries, although such contacts were still largely confined to Soviet bloc countries. Mongolia's 65 years of communism thus were a strange combination of tragedy, repression, and progress.

The Communist Philosophy

Communism is the political and economic expression of the Marxist-Leninist philosophy. Marxism-Leninism, developed by Karl Marx (1818–83) and Vladimir Ilich Lenin (1870–1924), is designed to improve the lot of the average working-class member of society, through state control of goods and services. It was developed in the 19th century in the industrial countries of Germany and Russia, where a small class of factory owners and landowners employed a large number of workers. Marxism-Leninism holds that the owners of enterprises (the capitalists) oppress the workers (the proletariat), paying them little and making them work in unpleasant or hazardous conditions, while the capitalists live a life of luxury. This was, in fact, a fairly accurate picture of life for many in the United States and Europe at the end of the 19th century, but it could also be pointed out that many capitalists had once been workers themselves, and it was possible to rise within the system. Marxist-Leninists would counter that even if those doing the exploiting had once been exploited, exploitation is still unjustified.

Marxist-Leninists believed that the proletariat should rise, overthrow the capitalists and the governments that permitted them to be oppressive, and take away the capitalists' wealth and distribute it equally among the people. Lenin, but not Marx, believed that only a dictatorship would have the ability to impose these changes. The Communist Party he helped found in Russia believed that it and government should control the distribution of money and resources, the economy, and the thoughts of its citizens in order to create a perfect socialist society.

The Communist System in Mongolia

The first communist constitution of Mongolia, the constitution of 1924, put some of these beliefs into practice. First of all, it set up a government structure modeled on the Soviet Union's, which with some tinkering remained in place for 65 years. The system purported to be slightly democratic in that it involved an election by the people of the country at one level of government. It gave the vote to everyone over 18 regardless of race, religion, or sex, provided the person lived by his or her own labor or was part of the army. Traders, moneylenders, former nobles, monks, and those who merely employed others were excluded from voting. But in practice the vote meant little, because the candidates were all determined by the Communist Party, called the Mongolian People's Revolutionary Party. Moreover, the government simply held new elections if it disliked the result, and the election system was very indirect. When office holders are indirectly elected, it means that they are not chosen by the people but by other officials elected by the people or even higher officials selected by other officials. The U.S. Senate was indirectly elected until the early 1900s. Indirect elections tend to result in elite, powerful, entrenched bodies that are not accountable to the people.

In Mongolia, officials elected by the people elected higher councils, which in turn elected the Great Khural, the nominal legislature of Mongolia. The Great Khural, in turn, elected a Little Khural, which acted as the executive between meetings of the Great Khural. The Little Khural, in turn, elected a Presidium, composed of five members, and a Council of Ministers, composed of 12 members. The Council of Ministers included the premier, the first deputy chairman, five other deputy chairmen, ministers, chairmen of the state committee, the chairman of the state bank, the president of the Mongolian Academy of Sciences, and the head of the Central Statistical Board. Complicated government structures that appear to have many different bodies contending for power, as in a democracy, are characteristic of Communist governments. Since, in the Mongolian system, all the bodies elected each other, however, they were not really in contention. The Communist Party controlled all of them. Having a large number of bodies also helped distribute power—at least in appearance—to a large number of people. In democracies, politicians enter and exit government service with elections. Under communism, there is only one political party, so all of the political leaders must be kept employed perenially by government. Finally, communism requires a huge bureaucracy because every aspect of life and the economy is controlled by the government rather than privately. In the United States, for example, large corporations such as General Mills, Cargill, and ADM, in addition to thousands of individual farmers and others, decide how much grain to produce and bring to market. In communist countries the government decides all of that. It is a huge undertaking.

The Communist government of Mongolia also included a judiciary system and a system of local governments. Members of the Supreme Court were elected by the Great Khural, for four-year terms. Hence, the judiciary did not have the separation from politics that many consider essential to the administration of justice. The Supreme Court presided over the provincial (*aymag*) and district (*soum*, plural *somon*) courts.

Mongolia was divided into 18 *aymag*, each with an assembly of people's deputies, and three autonomous cities—like Washington, D.C., not part of any state or *aymag*. Each *aymag* was divided into about 30 *somon*.

The legal system introduced and later implemented by courts and the legislature reflected the priority of the state over the individual. The most common crimes, according to a study done late in the Communist period, were theft and embezzlement of state property, black marketing, juvenile delinquency, misappropriation of materials, and speculation. Some of these "criminal" activities would be regarded simply as business in a capitalist society. "Black marketing" in Mongolia involved selling imported or other goods privately. "Speculation" only meant acquiring goods, such as cars, and selling them for a profit.

While punishment in general was no harsher than in America, crimes against state property were taken much more seriously than those against individual property. Theft of private property could land perpetrators in jail for five years, 10 years if carried out using force. Those who misused, abused, or stole *state* property could easily get seven years in jail and sometimes were put to death or given very long prison terms.

The Communist Economy

The constitution of 1924 also officially converted many of Mongolia's resources into communal government property, a process known as "nationalization." The constitution nationalized lands, mineral resources (such as oil and coal), forests, and water resources. It canceled all debts to foreign traders and abolished the private moneylending system within Mongolia. The Communists were threatened by private moneylenders in general and the Chinese traders in particular, but cutting off the ability to get loans also stifled any capitalistic impulses left in Mongolia. Without loans, it is practically impossible to build even a small business. The constitution also put the state in control of all foreign trade and declared the government's goal of depriving the monasteries of their power.

All these measures were said to have been initiated by Mongolians, but in reality the Soviets ran the show. Since the Soviet Union was embroiled in a power struggle following the death of Lenin, throughout the mid-1920s it did not initially have much time to implement the Mongolian constitution's decrees. It did, however, take a few immediate steps. In 1924, the Soviet-backed government introduced the first Mongolian currency, the tugrik. For the most part, Mongolians previously had used barter to obtain goods they could not produce themselves. They had traded items like livestock, tea, or salt for the items they needed. To the extent that they had used a modern form of money, it was usually a foreign currency. In conjunction with the issuance of the tugrik, the government established a state bank, Mongolbank. The government required that all state companies keep their money in it.

In the late 1920s, the Communist government began more serious economic reforms. Although it recognized that Mongolia was dependent upon the herding economy and had almost no experience with heavy industry, the Soviet economic model called for a movement away from pure nomadic herding to a more diversified, modern economy with farming and industrial sectors. The Mongolian government, therefore, launched government farms and plants to process animal products. It also gradually encouraged mining, exploitation of Mongolia's forests, and mass production of some consumer goods.

The government also turned its attention to the herding economy itself, hoping to run it on a more efficient and less individualistic model. It began by determining who had more livestock, wealth, and land than it thought they deserved. By 1931, more than one-third of the herding households had had their property seized and redistributed, a process called collectivization. The herders, accustomed to a great degree of control over themselves, their movements, and their property, responded angrily, slaughtering 7 million animals rather than give them up. This, combined with the failure of the newly organized herding collectives to operate properly, resulted in famine in the countryside in 1931–32. Mongolia came close to civil war. Only Mongolian and Soviet tanks and troops were able to suppress the rebellion.

The government, along with the Soviets, realized that it had been making changes too fast for the people to handle. Under the "New Turn," or "gradualist" policy, the government decided to change Mongolia more slowly, placing less emphasis on farming, relaxing state monopolies, and doing less to force herders to give up their private property right away.

The Purges

Temporarily abandoning collectivization did not mean, however, that the Communists were not bent on controlling the Mongolian people. Purges took place both within the government and Communist Party and outside it, in challenges to the noble classes' and monks' remaining power.

First, the Communist Party needed to clean its own house, getting rid of those who resisted Soviet influence or were economic moderates. Assassination was used as a political instrument. Such leaders of the revolution as Bodo, Chakdorjab, Togotkho, Puntsuk Dorji, Dindub, and 10 others were killed as early as 1922 for opposing Soviet control or welcoming Western influences on such things as clothing. Danzan, the vice premier, war minister, and commander in chief of the army, was shot with his associate in 1924 for disagreeing with another leader's stance on economic laws. Gendun, the prime minister from 1929 to 1937 and the architect of the "gradualism" policy, was executed in 1937. His pro-West, pro-freedom-of-religion views were his undoings. Choibalsan, Gendun's enemy, completed his rise to power at this time, becoming the premier and the minister of war simultaneously. Having vanquished his opponents within the government, he turned to the powerful classes in society that threatened communism as a whole.

The most powerful group prior to the revolution were the Buddhist monks. The government confiscated monastic property as part of the general process of collectivization described above, which occurred in phases. It also imposed very heavy taxes on the Buddhist church, denied it the role it had had in education, forbade it to recruit new monks, and outlawed the practice of all religion completely.

Even these harsh measures were not deemed to be sufficient by the government. In the 1930s, the government divided monks into three categories. Ordinary monks had to leave the monasteries and either become workers or join the army. Monks of middle and high status were regarded as more of a threat to the government and were sent to Siberian prison camps (where they often died). The highest-ranking monks were killed immediately. Reports estimate that of the 27,000 people the government executed between the revolution and 1939, 17,000 were monks. Only four of 700 monasteries survived.

In this process of breaking the power of the monasteries, the Communist government felt it should at least pretend to be just. Therefore, it interrogated the monks, tried to get them to condemn themselves, and conducted sham trials. Sharavjamts, a monk who lived through the purges, describes the experience (reproduced per the original):

> Investigators were working in shift not allowing me to sleep. No food or drink was given. After few days I could not speak becoming a live corpse. But I refused to pledge myself guilty because I was young and stubborn. At the end they were fed up and simply forced my fingertip on the interrogation record . . . [At the trial] I was sentenced to death with the execution within 24 hours. Every night they took away people, and brought new ones . . . Only after 26 days they . . . told [me] that the sentence was changed to ten years of prison.

Sharavjamts, obviously, was one of the lucky ones who escaped death. B. Dashtseden, now a journalist living in Ulaanbaatar, was studying at a rural school in 1937. One day he and a classmate became homesick and decided to walk 40 miles home for a visit. At one point on their journey, they came across tire tracks, which were unusual in the countryside, and decided to investigate.

> Grass was very thick and high, and we almost stumbled over a dead monk. He lay there with his stomach inflated . . . We were so terrified that immediately began to run back. But dead bodies in red and yellow attires [traditional monk clothing] were everywhere and we did not know where to run. I do not remember how long we ran and when got home. My mother told us never to mention to anyone about what we saw.

The Communists were determined to destroy almost everything associated with religion. Since the monasteries had enjoyed so much wealth and power, they were the repositories of most of the country's artworks. Treasures equal in Mongolia to Michelangelo's Sistine Chapel and Leonardo da Vinci's *Last Supper* were burned by the Communists. One monk described the fires at the Gandan monastery in Ulaanbaatar, probably the most important in Mongolia, as burning for several months continuously.

The daughter of Prime Minister Gendun, a victim of Communist purges, gestures at a painting of the bloodshed. (AP/Wide World Photos/Ng Han Guan)

Attempting to save even nonreligious art held by monasteries entailed great risk. Tudev Gombyn, as a young monk, took an oath to protect the spirit of Danzanravjaa, a renowned Buddhist teacher and poet who had lived in the 19th century and left behind precious drawings and manuscripts. In an attempt to save them from Communist destruction, he went to the abandoned Hamryn monastery night after night removing objects, placing them in boxes, and hiding the boxes in a number of caves. Even after filling dozens and dozens of boxes, Tudev had rescued only 10 percent of the treasures inside the monastery. At that point, the Communists demolished the monastery, sending the gold and silver sculptures of deities to the Soviet Union to be melted down. They used the stone from the monastery to build a town square in nearby Sainshand, Mongolia.

Tudev took care to protect those items he had saved. Every year, while supposedly out looking for medicinal herbs, he went to the mountains to check on the items. Once he was arrested, charged with the secret practice of religion, and imprisoned. Another time, the police actually found one of the caves and burned the art inside. Tudev could see the smoke from a distance. "When I found him," his grandson later recalled, "he was sitting on grass, crying and repeating, 'Why? It has nothing to do with religion, these are theater costumes only . . .'"

Power not formerly exercised by the monks was in the hands of the nobles, so the Communists determined to crush them as well. The Communists did so through depriving them of the vote, the ability to run in elections, and the ability to collect money or labor from those subject to them. They also crushed the nobility through executions. Choibalsan ordered some 900 nobles executed. Executions in addition to these may have gone unannounced.

Having stripped them of everything else, the Communists decided to strip nobles even of their names. These had signaled their high status and would have continued to do so for their descendants. While it was at it, the government decided to eliminate family names (what Americans call the last name, the name that connects you to your extended family) entirely, leaving Mongolians with only one name. This led to problems as innocent as confusion and as serious as inbreeding. Confusion, for example, resulted from the fact that 10,000 women might be named "Goldenflower," with nothing beyond that to tell them apart. Since the Communists also restricted travel and marriage between districts, Mongolians ended up marrying and having children with neighbors. Without family names to indicate that people were relatives, there was no way to prevent inbreeding. "In one place around here, none of the children was ever smart enough to graduate from school," a radio broadcaster, Naranchimeg, said after the Communist era ended. He implied that such was the result of inbreeding.

The Communists prohibited all mention of the most famous noble name, Genghis Khan, completely. The government prevented history museums from including Genghis in any exhibit. People were afraid to even say the name "Genghis Khan" for fear of being accused of committing a thought crime. The Communists were threatened by Genghis because he was the ultimate symbol of Mongolian power and freedom, and, incidentally, had conquered parts of the Soviet Union. Even completely nonthreatening aspects of Mongolian heritage came under fire. The Communists suppressed the traditional Mongolian script, requiring books and signs to be written using the Cyrillic (Russian) alphabet, despite the fact that they were in the Mongolian language. They also instituted a campaign to stop Mongolians from wearing the traditional *del*, a beautiful item of clothing well suited to the nomadic lifestyle (see chapter 8).

Industry and Internationalism

The most serious purges had ended by the conclusion of the 1930s, when the onset of World War II forced the USSR and Mongolia to turn their attention to military matters. Japan had taken control of Manchuria, historically connected to China, in the early 1930s, and by the late 1930s it was menacing Mongolia and the Soviet Union. By 1938, half of Mongolia's budget was spent on defense, and Soviet troops arrived in greater numbers. Mongolia's troops, too, massed on its border with Manchuria and beat back the Japanese in 1939. The Soviets signed a truce with Japan and turned their attention to their western front and Germany. Throughout the war, Mongolia supplied the USSR with livestock, clothing, money, and other contributions. About 10 percent of the Mongolian population, a very large percentage, was in uniform.

Choibalsan, who had presided over so much butchery during the purges, died in 1952, soon after the end of World War II. He was replaced as Mongolia's leader by Tsedenbal (1916–91), who held various titles including Communist Party general secretary, chairman of the Council of Ministers, and chairman of the Great Khural during his 32-year reign. Compared to Choibalsan, Tsedenbal was a moderate. He began his tenure by acknowledging the abuses and "personality cult" of Choibalsan, and implemented collectivization, industrialization, trade, and social progress less heavy-handedly and more effectively. During his regime, Mongolia also gradually opened diplomatic relations with countries other than the USSR in Europe and in Asia.

ECONOMIC CHANGES

Under Tsedenbal, the government finally implemented collectivization, this time peacefully. By 1958, almost all nomadic households belonged to a herding cooperative, or *negdel*. A herding cooperative was a governmental and economic unit, generally occupying an entire district of the country. It was further broken down into brigades, work teams, and *suurs*, or households. The *negdel* as a whole determined how many animals each household would have and how many animals it should give up for slaughter. The brigade decided how to manage pastures within the *negdel*. *Suurs* determined only how to manage grazing and the stock on an individual day.

The support system for members of *negdels* was also entirely controlled by the government. It took responsibility for providing veterinary care, help with hygiene, and entertainment to the *negdels*. Once a week, portable showers might be brought to a winter campsite for the benefit of the households. Troupes of performers, a few movies, and traveling stores sponsored by the government also made the rounds of the steppes. Instead of each family always having to load its *ger* on several camels' backs, the government provided trucks to transport them. It provided basic salaries, paid vacations, and health care to the herders regardless of how well the *negdel* performed. There were a few areas, however, in which individual initiative counted. Bonuses were available for keeping one's animals healthy, protecting them from wolves and death in the harsh climate and so forth. *Negdel* members were also allowed to keep a small number of animals of their own in addition to caring for those owned by the cooperative. If the animals they owned had offspring however, they would have to give up most of them to the cooperative, so there was not much chance to grow richer.

The government thus acknowledged the importance of nomadic life to the country and its economy but also wanted to encourage industrial development. As a symbol of this, the government replaced the "five snouts," or herding animals (see chapter 5), on Mongolia's national seal with a cogwheel and wheat sheaf, symbolizing industrialization and agriculture. Neither of these had been typically Mongolian, but the coal mining, electricity, and construction sectors in particular were growing throughout the postwar decades. The government built new industrial centers at Bayanhongor (coal mining, energy); Choibalsan (coal mining, meatpacking, food production, wool-scouring); Darhan (coal, construction materials); and Erdenet (copper and molybdenum mining, carpet manufacture, timber processing) in this period. Industrial production increased by more than 45 percent between 1971 and 1974 alone.

Soviet-controlled factories did bring technology to the nomad's existence. (Courtesy Library of Congress)

The communist economic system did manage to lead Mongolia from feudalism and toward some semblance of a 20th-century economy. But because such a system is based on the decisions of relatively few people and does not take advantage of humans' desire to compete in business, it is plagued by constant problems of inefficiency at worst and monotony at best. For example, in a capitalist economy, if stores are chronically short of shoes, someone is likely, on his or her own, to start making more shoes to meet the demand. Similarly, if the only shoes available are brown, poorly made, and uncomfortable, someone is likely to try making shoes in different colors or with better materials and styling. Under communism, none of this responsiveness is possible. The economy operates sometimes on one-year, but usually on three- or five-year, plans that dictate, for example, how many animals should be raised and killed to produce the leather for a determined number of shoes to be manufactured by a specified number of people paid a set amount of money. If any number in this complex chain is miscalculated, it is difficult to correct, and shortages result. Applying these economic principles meant, for example, that in Mongolia, with 20 million to 30 million animals and 2 million humans, people actually had to wait in line and cope with shortages of meat. Similarly, communist governments are not interested in coming up with shoe fashions or trying to satisfy people's desires for color, fun, and variety:

They are simply trying to satisfy people's *needs* in the most equitable way possible. And people, of course, do not actually *need* more than one color of shoe. Color and variety are also means of expressing individuality, which communism discourages.

SOCIAL CHANGES

Mongolia's Communist government was more effective in its efforts to improve the country's standard of living and social environment. Prior to the Communist era, for example, Mongolia had no paved roads whatsoever (by contrast, Illinois at one-tenth Mongolia's size had 5,434 miles of paved roads by 1926). The country's transportation system consisted of horse relay stations along old caravan routes (the same system in place in Genghis Khan's time). And whereas the United States by 1920 had more than 250,000 miles of railroad tracks, Mongolia had none. It also had no airports. With Soviet aid, the government began building roads, laying track, and eventually establishing air bases for the military and civilians. Progress was measurable but slow. As of the 1940s, 70 percent of freight was still carried by animals rather than motorized transportation. Even at the end of the Communist era, only 3 percent of the country's roads were paved, but this was better than nothing.

The Communist revolution also produced gains for women. Prior to the revolution, most women performed traditional household roles within the herding society. In general, they could not choose their husbands or divorce. The 1961 Criminal Code made it a crime to force a woman to marry or prevent her from marrying. The Communists also encouraged women to develop their skills and work outside the home. The 1961 Criminal Code also made it illegal to refuse jobs to pregnant women and mothers or prevent women from receiving an education.

In order to staff industry, road construction crews, and the military, Mongolia needed more people. In 1921, one-third of Mongolia's adult male population were monks. While not all monks kept their vow of celibacy, enough did that population decline became a serious problem. In addition to dismantling the monastic system, therefore, the government instituted measures to encourage childbearing. Those women and families who did not have children had to pay additional taxes; those who had large numbers of children were rewarded. A mother of five living children received a medal of the Order of Maternal Glory, Second Class, and a gift of 400 tugriks per child, per year. A mother of more than eight living children received a medal for the Order of Maternal Glory, First Class, and 600 tugriks per child, per year. In addition, these mothers got two-week, all-expenses-paid spa vacations and other discounts and benefits. A mother of many children could earn as much as a full-time factory worker.

The Communist government also drastically improved Mongolia's education system, hoping to encourage many to abandon the herding lifestyle for employment in industry. Before the revolution, such education as there was occurred in monasteries and, therefore, was not available to most Mongolians. Women could not become monks, and most herding families were too mobile to attend fixed centers of learning. As the Communists got rid of monasteries and their schools, they replaced them with nonreligious schools that were more accessible to most

Ulaanbaatar, meaning "Red Hero," was brought into the 20th century on a Soviet model. (AP/Wide World Photos)

Mongolians. Eight years of school were required, and 10 years were encouraged. Schools in rural areas permitted children of herders to board there so that they could remain in classes while their parents moved nomadically. After this elementary education, students had the option of attending vocational (industrial education) schools or secondary schools. Secondary schools offered training for office and professional work. Particularly good students could go on to receive specialized training in, for example, medicine. Many of the most promising students studied in Russia or other parts of the Soviet bloc. The Communist education system did not neglect adults either. The government sent teachers into people's homes to teach evening classes. It also encouraged ordinary citizens who were able to write to teach those who could not. This education system produced dramatic improvements. In 1941, approximately 90 percent of Mongolians could not read. By the end of the Communist era, 93 percent of adults were literate.

Women took particular advantage of the education system to rise from their former positions in society. Even as early as the 1930s, 35 percent of Mongolian judges were women, a far greater percentage than in the West. Fourteen of 33 members of the Mongolian legislature in 1940 were women. By the late 1970s, medicine in Mongolia had become dominated by women. As of 1985, toward the end of the Communist era, 63 percent of Mongolian students in higher education were women, as were 58 percent of the students in the specialized secondary schools.

Despite this apparent progress, social control continued, if less violently. In addition to the obvious economic controls of the herding cooperatives and employers in general, the government continued its efforts to suppress individuality and creativity. The arts, for example, remained a target. Western-style rock and pop were not allowed on state-run radio or TV. The only way Mongolians heard such music was on records and cassettes brought back by people who had traveled outside the country. Even if a Mongolian group had heard Western rock, it was not allowed to produce anything remotely like it. In fact, Mongolian musicians could rarely perform any of their own songs. They often were forced to write music to go along with lyrics written by the Mongolian Union of Writers, a government entity. These lyrics concerned acceptable topics such as the greatness of Mongolia and the Soviet Union and Mongolians' love of nature and their parents. Love between a man and a woman, that mainstay of Western rock, was considered too intimate for public performance. Singing about the wrong subjects could result in imprisonment.

The government exercised this control over musicians by controlling all access to performing spaces (there were not many available) and the activities of musicians when they were traveling abroad. "For example, when we were abroad, we couldn't go to the discos nor arrive at the hotel late. We couldn't go where we wanted. There were conflicts between the singers and musicians and the government representatives [sent to oversee the tour]. If I spoke to foreigners, I would be considered a spy," said D. Jargalsaikhan, now head of the Mongolian Singers' Association.

Maintaining such a wall against Western influences became more difficult as Mongolia gradually opened itself to the world. When China became the communist People's Republic in 1949, it and the USSR established friendly relations. Chinese aid and trade poured into Mongolia, and in 1956 the USSR actually withdrew all of its troops. Mongolia also established more connections with the rest of the world in this period. In addition to building trade relationships with other Soviet-bloc countries across the Eurasian continent, it joined the United Nations in 1961 and established diplomatic relations with Great Britain in 1963 and Japan in 1972. Soon, however, relations between the USSR and China deteriorated again; Soviet troops poured back in (100,000 as of the early 1970s); and once again Mongolia was in its familiar role as a buffer between opposing powers.

Despite these growing connections, Mongolia remained, by world standards, extremely isolated through the end of the Communist era. Even as of 1990, there were no credit cards in Mongolia. The only two places one could fly to from Mongolia were Beijing and Moscow. The Internet was of course unheard-of, and even international telephone calls were very difficult to arrange, plagued by static and breaks in the line. Even this level of isolation, however, was not enough to keep a democratic revolution out.

NOTES
p. 23 "While punishments in general . . ." UpInfo, "Incidence of Crime," in *Country Study and Country Guide for Mongolia.* Available on-line. URL: http://www.1upinfo.com/countryguidestudy/mongolia/mongolia172.html. Data as of June 1989.

p. 24 "The herders, accustomed . . ." Robert L. Worden, "Historical Setting," in *Mongolia: A Country Study* (Washington, D.C.: Library of Congress, Federal Research Division, 1991), p. 45.

p. 25 "Reports estimate . . ." Bradley Mayhew, *Mongolia* (Melbourne, Australia: Lonely Planet Publications Pty Ltd, 2001), p. 21.

p. 25 "Only four . . ." Mayhew, *Mongolia*, p. 43.

p. 26 "'Investigators were working . . .'" Quoted in "Witnesses Speak," in *Mongolia Today*, Issue 6. Available on-line. URL:http://www.mongoliatoday.com/issue/6/witnesses.html. Posted 1999–2002.

p. 26 "'Grass was very thick . . .'" "Witnesses Speak," in *Mongolia Today*, Issue 6.

p. 26 "One monk described . . ." "Witnesses Speak," in *Mongolia Today*, Issue 6.

p. 28 "'When I saw him . . .'" Quoted in "Sixth Guard of Priest's Spirit," in *Mongolia Today*, Issue 3. Available on-line. URL: http://www.mongoliatoday.com/issue/3/guard_priest.html. Posted 1999–2002.

p. 28 "'In one place around here . . .'" Quoted in "In Search of Sacred Names," in *Mongolia Today*, Issue 5. Available on-line. URL: http://www.mongoliatoday.com/issue/5/names.html. Posted 1999–2002.

p. 30 "Industrial production increased . . ." Worden, "Historical Setting," in *Mongolia: A Country Study*, p. 53.

p. 32 "By contrast, Illinois . . ." Mike Jackson, "Roarin' Road Buildin'," in *Illinois Issues*, March 2000. Available on-line. URL: http://www.lib.niu.edu/ipo/ii000327.html. Downloaded September 24, 2002.

p. 32 "And whereas the United States . . ." "Streamliners: America's Lost Trains," PBS Online. Available on-line. URL:http://www.pbs.org/wgbh/amex/streamliners/timeline/. Posted 1999–2000.

p. 32 "As of the 1940s . . ." Worden and Savada, eds., *Mongolia: A Country Study*, p. 163.

p. 32 "Even as of the end . . ." Keith Griffin, "Economic Strategy During the Transition," in *Poverty and the Transition to a Market Economy in Mongolia* (New York and London: St. Martin's Press, 1995), p. 2.

p. 35 "'For example, when we were abroad . . .'" Quoted in Peter Marsh, "Mongolia Sings Its Own Song," in *Ger Magazine*, Issue 1, September 9, 1998. Available on-line. URL: http://www.un-mongolia.mn/archives/ger-mag/.

PART II
Mongolia Today

3

DEMOCRACY AT LAST

Secretary-General Yumjaagiyn Tsedenbal's 32-year rule ended on August 23, 1984. While he was in Moscow, the Mongolian Politburo (ruling committee) replaced him. In explaining its decision, the Politburo falsely cited Tsedenbal's "health" and "consent." The new leader was Jambyn Batmonh (1926–), a 58-year-old professor, economist, and son of a herder. Batmonh had 13 years' experience in Communist governance.

Seven months later, in March 1985, Mikhail Gorbachev (1931–) rose to power in the Soviet Union and began instituting changes almost immediately. Some of these were internal: Gorbachev promoted *glasnost* (restructuring) and *perestroika* (openness) within his country. Some of his changes were external, involving a warming of relations with the United States, Europe, and nations in Asia. As relations with China improved, the USSR had less reason to use Mongolia as a buffer against Chinese attack. In July 1986, Gorbachev announced that the Soviet Union would begin withdrawing its 50,000 troops from Mongolia.

Encouraged by such developments, Secretary-General Batmonh began a parallel regime of *shinechel* (renewal) in Mongolia. Believing that capitalism and a modified form of socialism could coexist, Batmonh's government began instituting economic and political changes. It increased the number of animals that herdsmen were allowed to keep. It began allowing farmers to work their own small pieces of land instead of only government-owned land. It passed a law that gave factory directors more control over their businesses but still retained provisions for government

Rock music ushers in Mongolia's first multiparty election. (AP/Wide World Photos)

bailouts in the event that the factories could not compete in the market. The government also began acknowledging the abuses of previous Communist administrations.

But the pace of change allowed by the Communist government was not fast enough for Mongolia's citizens. As the desire for major changes was brewing in the fall of 1989, the rock band Hongk, meaning "bell," formed. Resisting the music censorship discussed in chapter 2, it wrote a song, "The Ring of the Bell," which was taped and copied and secretly passed from friend to friend:

> I had a nightmare last night
> As if a long arm tortured me,
> Strangling my words and blinding me.
> Luckily, the bell rang and woke me;
> The ring of the bell rouses us.
> The bell that woke me in the morning,
> Let it toll across the broad steppes,
> Reverberating mile after mile.

Let the bell carry our yearning
And revive all our hopes.

As a result of government incentives for having children, the population of Mongolia at this time was disproportionately young (70 percent was under age 30). Songs such as "The Ring of the Bell" were an extremely effective way of spreading the message of freedom among young people, and as protests grew, street concerts became an increasingly important element.

The protests grew despite the icy, cold December weather. Emboldened, musicians began performing protest songs publicly. At one performance, Hongk lowered a portrait of Genghis Khan over a stage to wild applause and dared to celebrate his accomplishments in the lyrics:

Forgive us for not daring
To breathe your name.
Though there are thousands of statues,
There is none of you.
We admired you in our hearts
But we dared not breathe your name.

The protests also had philosophical leaders such as 27-year-old Sanjaasuren Zorig (1962–1998). Until 1989, he was a soft-spoken lecturer in communist theory who lived with his mother. Both of his parents had been successful professionals under communism, and Zorig was actually half Russian. Nevertheless, he was inspired by reading about the protests in Eastern Europe. "Our population *has* awakened," Zorig told a reporter in January 1990 (emphasis added). "We have lost the feeling of groundless fear." Thus emboldened, he formed with others the Mongolia Democratic Association. It organized street protests, called for the resignation of the government, and went on a hunger strike to call attention to itself.

The government responded initially by waffling. At times it tolerated the protests, allowing leaders to air their demands on television. Other times it banned them. Batmonh himself was ambivalent, and factions within his government also disagreed on what to do. Some within the government supported the protests, such as Kinyatyn Dzardyhan, who became deputy prime minister in March 1990, and Boshigt, a doctor and a Communist Party leader who actually advised the young democrats. Others urged Batmonh to crush the demonstrators with tanks as the Chinese government had crushed protesters a few months earlier in Tiananmen Square in Beijing. During the climax of the protests, around March 5, 1990, troops actually were amassed at Ulaanbaatar stadium, only a 20-minute walk from the site of the protests. But Batmonh refused to send them, choosing resignation over violence. By the end of the month, Batmonh and the rest of the five-member Politburo had been replaced, and half the members of the larger Central Committee had offered to resign.

The existing constitution of Mongolia, written in 1960, had made the Communist Party the only legal political party. In May 1990, the constitution was amended to permit a multiparty political system and a presidential system that resembled those in the United States and Europe rather than those of communist countries. It also added a smaller, 53-member body to the existing 430-member Great Khural, Mongolia's legislature. Elections were scheduled for July of that year.

The campaign leading up to the 1990 election differed from those familiar to Americans. Instead of emphasizing their differences and attacking each other, the political parties each acknowledged the need for cooperation and communication with the other party. The newly formed democratic parties, which included the Mongolian Democratic Association, the National Progress Party, the Social Democratic Party, the Party of Free Labor, and the Green Party, largely united in acknowledging their inexperience in governing, lack of funding, and lack of name recognition by citizens. Meanwhile, the Communist Party, now known as the Mongolian People's Revolutionary Party (MPRP), recognized the need for reform of the political structure, foreign policy, and economy. It also promised seats in the legislature to the democratic opposition even if the opposition lost miserably, which in fact it did. Because of its support in the countryside, where people were less aware of the ferment in Ulaanbaatar, the MPRP won 85 percent of the seats in the Great Khural, the existing legislative house. It also won 62 percent of those in the Little Khural, the new legislative body. To ensure fairness, the elections were closely supervised by international observers.

More change was required. The initial amendment of the constitution had been minor, without adding the protections common in the constitutions of democratic countries. In 1991, a committee of members of the government and other experts began drafting a new, comprehensive constitution promising such protections.

The new constitution, signed January 13, 1992, provided for, for one thing, a greatly diminished role for the police force. In the Communist era the police force had been inseparable from the Communist Party. It had carried out the party's missions of quelling all opposition and monitoring citizens. This linkage was ended. The constitution also established the right to private property, although it maintained stronger government control over the economy than is common in the West. Article 6, clause 5 provides that "[t]he State shall regulate the economy of the country with a view to ensure the nation's economic security, the development of all modes of production and social development of the population." The constitution also provided that the "livestock of the country shall be national wealth and be subject to state protection," suggesting that privatization was not to be complete and immediate.

In contrast, and perhaps as a result of abuses throughout Mongolia's history, the constitution's provisions for human rights are far more extensively laid out than they are in the American Bill of Rights. They include such fundamental rights as those to freedom of speech, political association, and religion. More unusually, they include the right to a "healthy and safe environment," the "right to engage in creative work," equal rights for men and women, and the right to travel within the country.

The constitution still permits the government, however, to limit the right of citizens to travel outside the country "for the purpose of ensuring the security of the country and population and protecting public order." And even where the constitution protected rights, many Communist practices still survived in reality. At the time of the constitution's passage, for example, the government still controlled the amount of newsprint each newspaper received. Democratic opposition newspapers complained that the government gave more newsprint to the Communist Party's newspaper, allowing it to publish more often. The police force also retained the right to spy upon citizens "when necessary," a loose standard seeming to permit widespread wiretapping.

The 1992 constitution also established a new system of government, doing away with some of the structures created by the 1990 amendments to the previous constitution. It abolished the Little Khural completely and reduced the number of seats in the Great Khural to 76. Members of the Great Khural had to be at least 25 years old and elected by universal (all races, sexes, classes eligible) vote and secret ballot. Successful candidates won a four-year term.

The Great Khural, in turn, would select its own leadership: a chairperson, similar to the U.S. Speaker of the House, and a vice chairperson. These officials were to be chosen from the members of the Khural. It would also choose a prime minister, who is usually the leader of the party having or controlling the most seats in the Khural. The Khural would meet for at least 75 working days every six months. It is essentially a legislature, with much in common with the U.S. Congress, except that it also has some of the powers given to the president in the U.S. system. The Khural's powers include

- enacting, revising, and amending laws
- determining domestic and foreign policy
- ratifying or rejecting international agreements and/or treaties
- determining election dates for itself and the president
- determining its own standing committees (on topics like environment, law, budget)
- setting fiscal and tax policy and approving the national budget
- deciding the powers of the National Security Council
- recognizing the president after his election
- nominating/dismissing the prime minister
- declaring referendums
- declaring a state of emergency

The constitution also made changes to Mongolia's judicial branch. It created a court system including the Constitutional Court, the Supreme Court, *aymag* (provincial) capital city courts, *soum* (district), inter-*soum*, and specialized courts. The Constitutional Court exercises one of the functions of the U.S. Supreme Court: determining what the constitution means and whether laws passed by the Khural are in accordance with it. The Constitutional Court consists of nine members—three nominated by the Khural, three by the president, and three by the Supreme Court. This attempts to ensure that if one party controls one branch of government, for example the Khural, it will not have complete control over the interpretation of the laws it passes because it controls appointments to the Constitutional Court. However, judges on the Constitutional Court are not appointed for life, as are judges in the U.S. federal system, but only for six years. This may make them subject to political pressure.

The Supreme Court has 17 members, appointed by the president in consultation with the Khural and the General Council of Courts. The Supreme Court exercises functions similar to those of the U.S. Supreme Court outside of interpreting the constitutionality of laws: hearing appeals from lower courts; acting as the first court for some disputes, including those on human rights and misconduct by high-level officials; and interpreting the meaning of all Mongolian laws other than the constitution. The *aymag* (provincial) courts serve as courts of appeals for decisions from the local courts. They are also the court of first resort for more prominent cases—rape, murder, and grand theft, for example. The local courts hear mostly day-to-day civil and criminal cases.

Following the signing of the new constitution creating this governmental structure, elections were held in June 1992. Once again, the MPRP (the former Communist Party) triumphed, winning 71 of 76 seats, with 60 percent of the raw vote. The Democratic parties won five seats, with 40 percent of the vote.

Implementing the 1992 constitution, the Khural adopted the Law on Election of the Mongolian President and the Law on the Mongolian President in 1993. Under the law, presidential candidates must be at least 45 years old and have been resident in Mongolia for at least five years prior to the election. The president is elected to a four-year term and can run for reelection only once. Presidential duties include being commander in chief of the Mongolian army and chairman of the National Security Council. The president may veto the Khural's legislation, but the Khural can override a presidential veto by a two-thirds majority. Important, too, as well as problematical, the president has a say in the selection of the prime minister, the leader of the Great Khural. Under the constitution, the president presents the candidate for prime minister to the Great Khural for approval, although this is supposed to be done in consultation with the majority party in the Khural. Ochirbat, the incumbent Democrat, a nomad with a herd of 500 sheep, won the presidential election of 1993.

In the 1996 elections to the Khural, power changed hands. In a contest in which 90 percent of those eligible participated (a far better turnout than presidential elections ever garner in the United States, where only

50 percent of those eligible to vote participated in the 2000 presidential election), the alliance of the Democratic parties (the "DA") won 50 of the 76 seats. The MPRP won 25, and the UH(c)P (the United Heritage [conservative] Party) won one. This minority of one might have been insignificant but for the change in the Khural's internal rules requiring that two-thirds of the members be present in order to conduct business. Two-thirds of 76 is more than half way between 50 and 51, so 51 members were required. The UH(c)P decided to side with the MPRP and boycott the government, which made it impossible to act.

The next year, the Democrats got more bad news. Frustrated with rising poverty and unemployment, the electorate ousted President Ochirbat, replacing him with the MPRP candidate Bagabandi. Trying to consolidate their party to resist the former Communists, the next year the Democrats decided to put in new leadership in the Khural. Elbegdorj became the new prime minister. But this, too, failed to solve the deadlock. The Democrat-led government was trying to merge the state-owned Reconstruction Bank, which had gone bankrupt, with the privately owned Golomt Bank. Global institutions such as the International Monetary Fund had okayed the plan, but the MPRP opposed it. Some charged that Democrats had accepted loans from the bank as it was going bankrupt, when the bank should not have been making loans at all. The MPRP resorted to boycott once again, and now they had the president on their side as well. The MPRP, with the president supporting it, moved for a vote of no confidence in the Khural's leadership and won. Prime Minister Elbegdorj had to resign after only three months.

There followed, essentially, a constitutional crisis, such as is fairly common after new constitutions are ratified. In this case, the problem was in establishing who had the power to determine the would-be prime minister: the president, the majority party in the Khural, the Khural as a whole, or some combination? The constitution does give the president the right to present prime ministerial candidates to the Great Khural, but this seems to have been intended merely as a formality—otherwise the president could effectively prevent the Khural from functioning indefinitely. President Bagabandi ignored the intent and relied on the constitution's clear language, rejecting three candidates for prime minister a total of eight times in three months, from late July to early October 1998.

President Natsagiin Bagabandi, shown with his wife, A. Cyunbileg, in Switzer-land, 2002. (AP/Wide World Photos/Edi Engeler)

When Bagabandi tried nominating his own candidate, the DA turned the tables and rejected it. The one DA candidate accepted by Bagabandi was rejected by the Khural as a whole.

Later in October, another Democrat candidate, S. Zorig, was murdered. Zorig had been one of the heroes of the democratic revolution and an enemy of corruption. His killers have not been determined, but many believe Zorig was murdered because of his opposition to the opening of the Mon-Macau Casino in the basement of the Genghis Khan Hotel. The casino deal was found to be corrupt, and one month before the casino was to open, the plug was pulled on it. Three Democratic Khural members were eventually jailed for accepting bribes in connection with the deal. Some blame Zorig's death on his fellow Democrats, their business allies, or even organized criminals from Macau, a former Portuguese colony now part of China. Tens of thousands of Mongolians lined the streets for Zorig's burial procession, and a statue of him was placed outside the central post office in Ulaanbaatar in April 1999.

The government impasse was finally resolved when the Democrats agreed to President Bagabandi's proposal of J. Narantsatrait, mayor of Ulaanbaatar, as prime minister. He was approved in December 1998, but remained in office less than a year, until July 1999. Narantsatrait, too, was brought down in the wake of a scandal, this one involving the Erdenet Copper Mine, one of Mongolia's most important economic entities. He was replaced by R. Amarjargal, the fourth actual prime minister—among almost countless nominees—in less than a year and a half.

Parliamentary elections were held again in July 2000. The campaign was wild, featuring performances by Mongolian rockers and rappers and the Lipsticks (the "Spice Girls of the Steppe"). Election officials set up special ballot-box *gers* in the countryside, with herders riding a dozen miles on horseback to cast their votes. The MPRP won by a landslide, claiming 72 of 76 Khural seats and taking power away from the Democrats. Nambaryn Enkhbayar became prime minister. The MPRP's presidential candidate, Bagabandi, was reelected in 2001, for a second and final four-year term. The MPRP claimed that it was no longer a communist party, but did not plan to change its name because "there were no good names left."

Despite the structural problems and the voter dissatisfaction suggested by the swings in power, much was going well with the government, even at this time. Its specific changes in the areas of law and the economy will be dealt with in the chapters to follow, but its behavior, even with respect to itself—i.e., conducting fair elections, being open about its activities past and present—was a vast improvement on that of the Communist era.

The government has permitted a transparency unprecedented in Mongolia. The press lists, for example, all laws and decrees passed and adopted by the Khural in a given session. It also publishes tables showing the number of statements made and questions asked by each Khural member and the length of their remarks. This way, voters can tell whether their representatives are involved in important debates. The press also reports on the number of phone conversations and public meetings each Khural member has during the session, and how many letters from the public they receive (Khural members are expected to deal with issues raised in such letters within a month of receiving them). Many, especially Westerners, believe that Mongolians deserve even more openness from government, however. Globe International, funded by the U.S.

embassy in Mongolia and AusAID, an Australian group, has launched a group called The Public's Right to Know Freedom of Information. It aims to draft laws for passage by the Khural that implement the constitution's guarantees of government openness. It also plans to run a campaign and produce a handbook to raise public awareness. "Many people do not understand that in a democratic society people have the right to access information and demand that government is open and transparent," said Globe coordinator J. Tuul.

The government, although not tied to those ordering the purges of the 1920s and 1930s, decided to take responsibility for them. Every year, on September 10, it holds a memorial service for the politically oppressed of that era. Although people were executed throughout the Communist era, September 10, 1937, was a particularly brutal day. Sixty-nine people were accused of being Japanese spies or otherwise allegedly disloyal. Also on that day, Prime Minister Gendun and Military Marshal Demid were arrested. Relatives of all victims of political repression, as well as state leaders and representatives of various organizations, lay wreaths at the memorial site on the anniversary day, and religious leaders conduct a service.

The government also takes more than symbolic action. In the 1990s, the Khural passed a law on the Exoneration and Compensation of Politically Repressed People. The government has gone through the records of those convicted of political crimes and sentenced to death or imprisonment and officially absolved them of guilt. More than 30,000 people have had their names cleared in this manner. The government also began giving homes and money to surviving victims of political repression or their spouses, if the victims were dead. More than 400 *gers* and apartments have been given away through this program. From 1998 until the program was temporarily halted for lack of funding (it was expected to begin again), 14,000 people received a total of more than $11 million (or 11 billion tugriks) in compensation for past suffering. These grants amount to between $500 and $1,000 per family. Sixteen thousand additional potential victims are waiting for their applications for assistance to be processed.

Challenges to government's honesty and effectiveness also remain, however. Corruption was alive and well in Mongolia even at the end of 2002, according to reports. In August, a Japanese investigation revealed that employees of the Japanese company Mitsui & Co. had bribed a high Mongolian official in order to help the company win an energy contract from the Mongolian government. The Mongolian official was in the Energy Coordination Office of the Infrastructure Ministry. He accepted more than 1 million yen ($8,400) in exchange for providing information on what the ministry expected to pay for the energy contract and other information helpful to Mitsui in making a bid. In fact, Mitsui did win the contract for first-phase construction of 150 power generation facilities in 73 Mongolian villages.

Corruption still affects small business as well as large. One small shoe-factory owner wishes that he could expand and produce higher quality shoes that would be of interest to urban Mongolians as well as townspeople. He blames economic stagnation in part on the fact that the average Mongolian cannot get a loan without bribing someone.

The judiciary and police have also failed occasionally to live up to their duty of protecting the constitution, enforcing law, and preventing crime. As discussed above, the constitution of 1992 is highly protective of civil rights. It guarantees due process for those arrested, searched, or detained by the police. In America, due process requires police, for example, to have probable cause and a warrant to do most searches, people may not usually be held without being charged with a crime, and the police may not physically torture people to obtain confessions. Mongolia has incorporated protections like these into its criminal code of law, but problems remain. Many citizens are not aware that they have rights of this nature and so do not assert them. Others may be prevented from doing so. In 2002, for example, it was alleged that five people accused of murdering a shopkeeper in 1999 had been tortured for two years while in custody in order to force a confession from them. One died of tuberculosis, and the other four claimed that they had been subjected to electrical shocks, threats against their families, and other grotesque practices. A joint monitoring commission dismissed these allegations of abuse, but the Supreme Court ordered that the case be investigated again. Even in the absence of torture, many allege that they have been subject to arrest and detention without cause.

Crime has, in fact, risen since the transition to democracy, and some say the government, including the courts, is not doing enough to stop it. Although organized crime is nowhere near as serious a problem as in neighboring China and Russia, for example, it is involved in the drug trade and prostitution. At a May 2002 meeting of the Council on Crime Prevention, the Chiefs of Criminal Police and Crime Prevention reported that serious and organized crime had increased 61 percent in 2001 over previous years. In a country of 2.5 million people, 4,000 crimes were registered in 2001. This figure included 372 murders. The *ger* districts of cities—centers of poverty—are also crime centers, with people being killed over things like video games and food. People complain that the government has done little to improve conditions in these places. In 2001, 55.1 percent of thefts, 63.1 percent of acts of hooliganism, and 57.5 percent of murders were committed by unemployed people. Child abuse and child labor are also problems; some women seeking employment outside Mongolia have become victims of trafficking. Recently, the government established a National Commission on Human Rights, which published a report critical of the government. Efforts to improve are ongoing.

NOTES

p. 41 "'I had a nightmare . . .'" Quoted in Nicholas D. Kristof, "A Mongolian Rock Group Fosters Democracy," in *New York Times*, March 26, 1990.

p. 41 "'Forgive us for not daring . . .'" Quoted in Nicholas D. Kristof, "A Mongolian Rock Group Fosters Democracy," in *New York Times*, March 26, 1990.

p. 41 "'Our population has awakened . . .'" Quoted in Graham Hutchings, "Mongolia Stirs Under Glasnost," in *Daily Telegraph*, January 28, 1990.

p. 48 "'there were no good . . .'" Mayhew, *Mongolia*, p. 30.

p. 49 "'Many people do not . . .'" Quoted in "Freedom of Information," in *Mongol Messenger*, September 11, 2002. Available on-line. URL: http://www. mongolnet.mn/mglmsg/.

p. 50 "He accepted more than one million . . ." "High Level Corruption Revealed," in *Mongol Messenger*, September 11, 2002. Available on-line. URL: http://www.mongolnet.mn/mglmsg/.

p. 50 "In fact, Mitsui did win . . ." "Japanese Trading House Bribes Mongolian Official to Win Aid Contract," on Xinhua New Agency Website, August 28, 2002. Available on-line: URL: http://news.xinhuanet.com/english/2002-08/28/content_541361.htm.

p. 50 "He blames economic . . ." Pekka Mykkanen, "Mongolia's Bumpy Road to Economic Development," in *Helsingen Sanomat*, August 13, 2002. Available on-line. URL: http://www.helsinkihs.net/news.asp?id=20020813IE10.

p. 50 "In 2002, for example . . ." U.S. Dept. of State—Bureau of Democracy, Human Rights and Labor, "Country Reports on Human Rights Practices: Mongolia," March 4, 2002. Available on-line. URL:http://www.state.gov/g/drl/rls/hrrpt/2001/eap/8357.htm. Posted March 4, 2002.

p. 51 "At a May, 2002 meeting . . ." "Organized Crime Up 61 Percent in Mongolia," in *BBC Monitoring International Reports*, May 15, 2002.

p. 51 "The *ger* districts of cities . . ." Michael Kohn, "Uncharted: Ulaanbaatar, Mongolia: Macarena in the Middle of Nowhere," in *Student Traveler Magazine*. Available on-line. URL: http://www.studenttraveler.com/mag/09-99/ mongolia.cfm. Site updated September 23, 2002.

p. 51 "In 2002, 55.1 . . ." "Organized Crime Up 61 Percent in Mongolia."

4

THE ECONOMICS OF
TRANSITION

It is impossible to discuss Mongolian government in the 1990s without also discussing the Mongolian economy. Despite some past and continuing snags, particularly problems with corruption, democracy came relatively easily to Mongolia. Elections were judged to be fair from the outset. If the Mongolian government does not embrace separation of powers between its executive, legislative, and judicial branches to the extent the United States does, neither does Britain, whose legislative and judicial branches overlap. The transition to capitalism has been much more difficult. Mongolia had no industrial economy prior to the Soviet occupation, so what industry and development the Soviets brought was in many senses artificial. The goods Mongolian factories made did not actually have to compete on the open market; they only had to be transported across the border to the Soviet Union and into the hands of consumers who had as little choice about buying the goods as Mongolians had about making them. The machinery, the spare parts, and the energy to run Mongolian factories were provided by the Soviets. So was the know-how to run them. Even if Mongolians had been able to remember how they ran their own economy 65 years earlier, it would not have helped much. In the early 1920s, Mongolia was operating much as Europe had 500 years earlier: a poor model for entering the global economy at the close of the 20th century. Not surprisingly, few knew what to do, and Mongolia suffered many of the same problems of poverty, confusion, and unemployment suffered by Eastern Europe at about the same time. This suggests that if the government made mistakes in running the economy, they at least were easy ones to make.

Economic woes began soon after the withdrawal of the Soviets and with the transition to democracy. Within a year, the country's economy experienced three shocks: one caused by the withdrawal of Soviet aid, one caused by the withdrawal of Soviet economic advisers, and one caused by a sudden suspension of trade. To each in turn. The Soviet aid, which had been considerable, was reduced in 1989 and terminated in 1991. Soviet advisers had essentially run the economy for 65 years, bringing Mongolia out of feudalism. Soviet trade had been based on the barter system, with Mongolians exchanging livestock, livestock products, and minerals for Soviet machinery, oil, and finished goods. Beginning in 1991, the Russians started insisting on hard (stable, foreign—that is, not Mongolian) currency for their wares, which Mongolians could not come up with. Oil stopped flowing; spare parts needed for repairs of Soviet machinery stopped coming; and even specialty foods needed for dishes on restaurants' menus were gone. Trucks, buses, power stations, agricultural equipment, and the construction industry simply stopped running. This only made Mongolia less able to come up with the needed hard currency. If shop shelves had been monotonous under communism, they were empty now. The collapse was considered equivalent to the sudden loss of half the nation's expenditures. Unemployment, before almost unknown in Mongolia, soon followed. In Dornod *aymag,* in southeast Mongolia, unemployment reached 60 percent.

At the same time, the government was trying to stimulate the economy or at least lay the groundwork for future growth by implementing market reforms. One of these was privatizing business, that is, ending government ownership. It began in 1991, before the new constitution had even been passed, and operated through a system somewhat like a board game, which might have been amusing if the prosperity of a nation had not been at stake. The government distributed two colors of free vouchers to the entire population. There were red ones, to use in bidding at auction for entire small companies, and blue ones, to buy shares in large formerly state-run enterprises. The vouchers could also be sold among citizens. By the close of 1993, 2,440 small and 797 large enterprises had been privatized—an amazing number. The process would seem to have accomplished a complete turnover of the national wealth to the people, but the initial results were not as dramatic as they might appear. At least in the case of the large companies, no one citizen initially owned much of any company. Besides, citizens were unfamiliar with the concept of stockholders' rights or derivative lawsuits (lawsuits against company management, usually), and so essentially left the company they now partly owned to be managed by those who had always done so. Since very few companies were doing well, there were few profits to distribute to shareholders. The government also retained significant ownership of the large enterprises. Thus, at first, privatization did not do much good for the country.

At the same time, livestock was privatized, that is, animals were given to individual herders. Now competitive with each other where before they had been in cooperatives, herders had three possible options open to them: (1) try to increase the size of their herd vs. others, (2) improve the quality of their animals, or (3) develop animal processing capabilities so they could sell finished products for a high price. The third option requires organization, business skill, and large amounts of money. The second requires skill in animal care and breeding. The first requires money alone. Most herders chose the first, and flocks quickly grew, from 25 million to 30 million. But the system that had helped keep what animals there were alive was allowed to break down (see chapter 5, "Dzud"). For example, the ability to graze animals in the southern part of the country, near the Gobi Desert, depends on the functionality of water wells there, since there is so little water above ground. Well maintenance dropped by the wayside, and by 1999, only 20 percent of the 24,600 wells remained operational. This resulted in about a third of the pastures in Mongolia being unusable, which, combined with increased herd size, put great pressure on the other two-thirds of Mongolia's land. In addition, veterinary and transportation services declined. Herders have seldom been rich, but many felt that things had been better in the Soviet era. Despite having 20 sheep, 30 goats, and 10 cows, more than her family had under communism, one herder spoke to her family's depression. "Life is getting worse . . . We have just enough to feed ourselves because flour and rice are so expensive and the money for goat hair [probably meaning cashmere] is so little now." Her husband blamed conditions on people's laziness, a holdover from the Communist era when they did not make economic decisions for themselves and lacked incentives to be productive. "Mongolians are lazy. They don't want to improve themselves, that's the problem."

In addition to distributing state assets, the government quickly took the important step of "liberalizing" prices. Under communism, prices were not determined by the amount of demand versus the amount of supply—that is, the "market," under capitalism. Rather, they were set by economic planners. In comparison with the rest of the world, they were artificially low. In order to participate in the global financial system and become a market economy, the government needed to stop setting prices and let the market determine them. So prices of certain goods were freed, that is, raised, in 1990. By 1992, the great majority of retail prices were liberalized. In the same spirit of reality, the Mongolian currency, the tugrik, was devalued in 1991 to reflect its true lack of buying power. At the same time, the government was overly willing to extend credit to people, or allow them to borrow money in other ways. Inflation, or an even more rapid devaluation of currency caused in part by oversupply, soon followed, reaching 325 percent in 1992 (this essentially means that an item purchased, for example, for $40 at the beginning of the year would cost $130 if bought a year later). Inflation, besides being dispiriting and decreasing buying power, discourages people from saving any money. This then makes it difficult for companies to get people to invest in them, which in turn makes it difficult for the economy to grow. The Mongolian economy became completely chaotic and dysfunctional. The country was kept running only through foreign aid.

Foreign aid, in a variety of forms, did pour in. Russia suspended repayment obligations on the large debt Mongolia owed it, despite having huge economic problems of its own. Aid from western countries and international financial institutions grew from $4.7 million in 1990 to $80.8 million in 1991 to $299.2 million in 1992, back slightly to $104.2 million in 1993. This aid came in the form of money and technical assistance. Trade with the West also brought in many newer, high-quality goods. All of this aid, however, could not keep Mongolians from sinking quite far into poverty. Most believe the Mongolian government used the money unwisely to prop up struggling state enterprises when they probably should have been left to live or die by the market. The government also used foreign aid to fund Mongolians' continued consumption when, according to some economists, they should have been accommodating themselves to the economic reality of higher prices and learning to save money. Many economists believe Mongolia should have used the money to invest in new businesses, stimulating others to invest. So disappointed were lenders that the Asian Development Bank, the World Bank, and the International Monetary Fund all temporarily suspended lending in mid-1992. Even three years later, Mongolia was still not able to borrow money through the ordinary channels that countries with good credit are able to use.

In short, many believe that though Mongolia made a lot of changes quickly, it did not make them quickly enough. It privatized some companies but propped up those it either thought were important or had political connections to. It liberalized many prices but favored certain industries with tax credits and subsidies while seeming to punish others. Food prices, for example, were not liberalized initially—probably to protect the consumer from starvation. But when prices of other commodities were rising while foodstuffs remained low, herders and farmers had little incentive to increase or maintain their production because they could earn so little from it. For a market to work efficiently, all of its elements must be subject to its laws.

Similar problems of incomplete privatization and relics of Communist-era cronyism plagued the banking sector, which is so essential to the growth of any modern economy. The banking crisis that brought down Elbegdorj's government (see chapter 3, page 46) was just one of those plaguing Mongolia in the late 1990s. As the Reconstruction Bank went down, giant companies crucial to the viability of Mongolia's economy were struggling to close their accounts with it and transfer money to the more trustworthy, also state-owned Trade and Development Bank. The Golomt Bank, the subject of the scandal, was actually the only private bank that was financially sound at the time. Many others had gone down by making foolish or corrupt loans, often to friends or relatives of bank employees. State banks had continued to make loans to companies friendly to politicians, despite poor credit. Even those banks still afloat were completely dysfunctional by Western standards. When a company that supposedly had substantial funds in its account wished to make a withdrawal to pay employees' salaries, it would often have to give its bank a week's notice to find the money. Mongolia also lacked a system comparable to the United States's Federal

Deposit Insurance Corporation, which insures deposits in bank accounts up to $100,000. Every time a bank failed in Mongolia, therefore, many people lost savings. The central bank, Mongol Bank, in an effort to restore confidence, started suing those who failed to pay back loans and asking local newspapers to publish the names of bad debtors. Shaming people is a common enforcement tactic in tight-knit Mongolia; failure to pay one's cable bill can also get one's name on TV.

But such responses did little to convince Mongolians to trust banks with their money. Instead, many opted to convert as much money as they could into foreign ("hard") currencies and stash it at home. Mongolia also developed an informal, small-time "banking" system based on trust and collateral that would have been at home in Europe in the 1600s. Collateral is something offered to a lender in the event that a loan is not paid back. In Mongolia, entrepreneurs would run small currency-exchange businesses, taking a commission; offer weekly to year-long loans, taking jewelry or cars as collateral; or provide loans at extremely high interest rates. Pawn shops were everywhere. An informal system such as this is creative and better than nothing, but it is insufficient to support a modern, growing economy.

Despite the struggles, Mongolia has begun to reap some of the rewards of having established a market economy. Between 1989 and 1999, more than 10,000 new private businesses opened. By 1998, 430,000 people (about one-fifth of the country, and a larger fraction of those old enough to work) were working for privately owned businesses. Eighty percent of the new jobs being created were in the private, nongovernmental sector.

Some people have thrived under privatization by converting skills acquired under communism into moneymaking businesses. Under communism, L. Bayasgalan, trained as a microbiologist, did government-sponsored research on fungus. In 1990, taking a gamble, she left to build an organic vegetable business in a country that previously had shunned vegetables. She began by farming her family's vegetable plot outside Ulaanbaatar with her father. By the late 1990s, she had three employees and was delivering broccoli, rhubarb, onions, lettuce, tomatoes, cucumbers, spinach, turnips, cauliflower, and five types of cabbage to market. "Since I am delivering the products, I know what the customers want," Bayasgalan said. "A lot of the old state-run companies don't enjoy this efficiency. There are too many people doing not enough work."

The Mongolian Women Farmers' Association (MWFA) is trying to nurse similar growing and entrepreneurial skills through its community service activities. The *ger* districts—areas of Ulaanbaatar where people live not in modern apartment buildings but in clusters of traditional housing—are among the centers of poverty and desperation in the country. Some of the *gers* do, however, have yards, and MWFA is training their owners to turn them into small-scale farms and gardens. The group has turned one *ger* into a vegetable, pig, and chicken demonstration farm, training center, and soup kitchen. It also trains hundreds of families to be more self-sufficient themselves even while living in the city.

Others have parlayed skills acquired as black-market traders during communism into even wilder success. B. Jargalsaikhan was a cashmere factory employee by day and an illegal goods trader by night under communism. He traveled across Europe and Asia dealing in luxuries unavailable to Mongolians—perfume, jeans, watches and electronics, and pop records. He kept half his money in foreign banks, the other half in drawers in his apartment. Jargalsaikhan was twice arrested for "possessing money," but luckily was released both times. The stash came in handy when he started the Buyan Cashmere company in 1989. He grew from six employees to more than 900. He claims to be Mongolia's first millionaire, tools around Ulaanbaatar in a Land Cruiser or Humvee, and sports Italian suits.

Y. Enkhee, who likes to be known as "Eddie," has had similar success, by borrowing a model from the West. He opened a chain of pizza restaurants with delivery service in Ulaanbaatar, a restaurant-starved city under communism. Unlike many Mongolian menus, which are confined to varieties of mutton, Enkhee offers 16 kinds of pizza. Some are Western in taste; the "Pizza Mongolia," on the other hand, has chunks of fatty mutton on it. Where service in the old Soviet-style restaurants is either non-existent or sluggish, that at Enkhee's Pizza del La Casa chain is fast.

Thus, the gap between rich and poor is very wide in Mongolia. Politicians, the ones who created the privatization scheme, often profited from it. Many Mongolians were willing to sell their vouchers for very little because they had gotten them for free. Those who were able to buy vouchers from others now own large shares of corporations, while the average citizen has little. The rich enjoy a lifestyle that would not be unfamiliar to Westerners. They are able to afford cell phones, cars, fancy clothes, and meals at restaurants in Ulaanbaatar serving foreign cuisine. The poor have almost nothing. In a recent poll, only 10 percent of Mongolians said life was better since the transition to democracy and capitalism. Half said it was the same, and 30 percent said it was worse.

Hope for the Mongolian economy as a whole comes from the mining and agriculture sectors—the former being a relatively new industry in the country, the latter, one as old as the hills. Mining currently accounts for about one-third of Mongolia's gross domestic product. In addition, it is an important source of hard currency because most minerals are exported. Mongolia has more than 300 active mines. Coal reserves are estimated at more than 100 billion tons. Seventy-five gold mines produce thousands of pounds per year, which sell for hundreds of dollars per *ounce*. The copper mine and processing plant at Erdenet, one of the largest copper mines in the world, earns Mongolia $900 million per year. In addition, the country is responsible for 15 percent of the world's output of fluorspar. It mines uranium, tungsten, and zinc as well (see also chapter 5). As of 2001, Mongolia had no active oil fields, but recent explorations suggest that it might have reserves of up to 5 billion barrels. Mongolia may also be able to collect transit fees for oil piped across it from Russia and other former Soviet republics to China and East Asia. In general, experts say that Mongolia is one of the least "dug out" countries in the world, meaning that most of its territory has yet to be explored with the aim of mineral exploitation.

Herding also accounts for about one-third of the Mongolian economy. Cashmere, meat, and hides represent, after copper from Erdenet, the largest source of foreign currency. Cashmere alone, as of 2001, accounts for 15 percent of Mongolia's gross domestic product, or the total value of all goods and services produced in the country in a year. It is the world's second-largest producer (behind China). Mongolia's dearth of processing capacity hurts it, however. It enables Chinese merchants to name their price for the raw cashmere and then earn money from finishing it into sweaters, and so forth. Also, the price of cashmere fell by 65 percent throughout the 1990s.

Challenges to continued economic improvement include a grossly inadequate transportation system and an unreliable power supply. A still-undeveloped legal and regulatory system also makes foreign investors wary. They wonder if they will have to compete with heavily subsidized or inadequately supervised competitors and whether they will be able to successfully sue for damages if local suppliers or customers breach contracts. The small size of Mongolia's market for goods (the entire country's population is equivalent to that of Minneapolis–St. Paul) also discourages foreign investment. So does corruption, which rears its head in the corporate world as well as in government. In August 2002, the president of the Tsagaan Shonkhor Company, Ch. Enkhtaivan, received an eight-year prison sentence for his involvement in a violent and dirty corporate battle. Enkhtaivan had been charged with beating two men associated with and blackmailing the director of Tas, another Mongolian entity, in order to win 51 percent of the shares in a ship, the *Sukhbataar*. He also was charged with, following his arrest on the former charge, bribing a police chief to let him out of jail.

Efforts to improve the banking system were somewhat more promising as of 2002. In that year, the government decided to privatize the Trade and Development Bank, one of the more successful state-run banks. For the first time in the sale of a state asset, it was decided to open bidding for shares in the bank to international entities. By doing this, the government hoped to increase foreign trust and involvement in Mongolia's economy. Banca Commerciale Lugano of Switzerland and Gerald Metals (U.S.-based) bought 76 percent of the bank for $12.23 million, while 24 percent remained in the hands of the bank's employees and other Mongolians. The foreign buyers also promised to invest $28 million in the bank in 2003 and 2004. In addition, ING Bank of the Netherlands will provide assistance in managing the bank.

As of 2002, although many large economic entities are still state-controlled, the private sector accounts for more than 70 percent of the gross domestic product. Inflation now remains below 12 percent, and unemployment was at about 17 percent at last measure. The country is still extremely poor by world standards, having a per capita annual income of about $405. Prices are also still low, however, so this number is not *quite* as dismal as it sounds. For comparison, going to see a Hollywood movie only costs about $1 in Mongolia, as opposed to $7–$10 in the United States. But Mongolia's economy continues to rely heavily on foreign aid.

NOTES

p. 54 "Within a year . . ." Keith Griffin, "Economic Strategy During the Transition," in *Poverty and the Transition to a Market Economy in Mongolia* (New York and London: St. Martin's Press, 1995), pp. 5–6.

p. 54 "The collapse was considered . . ." Mayhew, *Mongolia*, p. 31.

p. 54 "In Dornod *aymag* . . ." Mayhew, *Mongolia*, p. 31.

pp. 54–55 "By the close of 1993 . . ." Griffin, "Economic Strategy During the Transition," p. 10.

p. 55 "Thus privatization . . ." Griffin, "Economic Strategy During the Transition," p. 12.

p. 55 "Now competitive . . ." "White Death Strikes Again," in *Mongolia Today*, Issue 5. Available on-line. URL: http://www.mongoliatoday.com/issue/5/dzud.html. Posted 1999–2002.

p. 55 "Most herders . . ." Conor O'Clery, *Irish Times*, "The Dark Side of Mongolia," in *Mongolia Today*, Issue 2. Available on-line. URL: http://www.mongoliatoday.com/issue/2/dark_side_1.html. Posted 1999–2002.

p. 55 "Well maintenance . . ." "White Death Strikes Again," in *Mongolia Today*, Issue 5. Available on-line. URL: http://www.mongoliatoday.com/issue/5/dzud.html. Posted 1999–2002.

pp. 55–56 "Life is getting worse . . ." and "Mongolians are lazy . . ." Quoted in O'Clery, "The Dark Side of Mongolia."

p. 56 "Inflation, or . . ." Guek-Pang Cheng, *Mongolia* (Tarrytown, New York: Marshall Cavendish, 1999), p. 51.

p. 56 "Aid from . . ." Griffin, "Economic Strategy During the Transition," p. 6.

p. 57 "So disappointed . . ." Griffin, "Economic Strategy During the Transition," p. 8.

p. 57 "In short, many believe . . ." Griffin, "Economic Strategy During the Transition," pp. 7–8.

p. 58 "Every time a bank . . ." "Mongolia's First Private Bank Fails," in *The Financial Times*, July 12, 1996.

p. 58 "Mongolia also developed . . ." G. Enkhtuya, "Depositors' Blues: Banks Fail to Reform and Become Solvent," in *Ger Magazine*, Issue 2, May 12, 1999. Available on-line. URL: http://www.un-mongolia.mn/archives/ger-mag/.

p. 58 "Between 1989 . . ." Guek-Cheng, Pang Mongolia (Tarrytown, New York: Marshall Cavendish, 1999), p. 40.

p. 58 "Eighty percent . . ." Michael Kohn, "Young Mongolian Entrepreneurs Lead the Business Revolution," in Ger Magazine, Issue 2, May 12, 1999. Available on-line. URL: http://www.un-mongolia.mn/archives/ger-mag/.

pp. 58–59 "'Since I am delivering . . .'" Kohn, *Ger Magazine*, Issue 2, May 12, 1999.

p. 59 "The group has turned one . . ." "Organic Business," in *Mongol Messenger*, September 3, 2002. Available on-line. URL: http://www.mongolnet.mn/mglmsg/index.html. Site updated September 26, 2002.

p. 59 "B. Jargalsaikhan was . . ." *Mongol Messenger*, September 3, 2002.

p. 59 "Y. Enkhee . . ." *Mongol Messenger*, September 3, 2002.

p. 60 "In a recent poll . . ." Mayhew, *Mongolia*, p. 24.

p. 60 "Cashmere alone . . ." Mayhew, *Mongolia*, p. 31.

p. 60 "It is the world's . . ." Trade Environmental Database. "TED Case Studies: Globalization of the Cashmere Industry in Mongolia." Available on-line. URL: http://www.american.edu/TED/mongolia.htm. Downloaded September 25, 2002.

p. 61 "In August 2002 . . ." "Jail for Centre Point Gang," in *Mongol Messenger*, September 11, 2002. Available on-line. URL:http://www.mongolnet.mn/mglmsg/.

p. 61 "In 2002, the government decided . . ." Associated Press, "Mongolia Sells Majority Bank Stake," in *Mongolia News*, May 21, 2002. Available on-line. URL: http://cgi.wn.com/?action=display&article=13716417&templatee=mongolianews/indexsearch.txt&index=recent. Site updated September 25, 2002.

p. 61 "Inflation now remains . . ." Asian Development Bank, "Mongolia's Economic Growth Expected to Nudge Upwards in 2002," April 9, 2002. Available on-line. URL:http://www.adb.org/Documents/News/2002/nr2002040.asp.

p. 61 "The country is still . . ." U.S. Department of State, Bureau of Democracy, Human Rights and Labor, "Country Reports on Human Rights Practices: Mongolia," March 4, 2002. Available on-line. URL: http://www.state.gov/g/drl/rls/hrrpt/2001/eap/8357.htm. Posted March 4, 2002.

p. 61 "For comparison . . ." Mongolia Street Connection, "Have Your Say." Available on-line. URL: http://mongolia.worldvision.org.nz/yoursay/yoursayans. asp?category=1&page=4. Posted March 9–April 1, 1999.

5

THE ENVIRONMENT

Land influences culture in every country, but perhaps in none more so than in Mongolia. It seasoned Genghis Khan; it attracted Russia and China with its emptiness and position; and it still provides half of Mongolians with their livelihood (see chapter 6). It is beautiful, fruitful, stark, strange, and one of the last hosts to some of the rarest animals in the world.

With a population of only 2.5 million in a country of 600,000 square miles, Mongolia's population density is a low 4.2 persons per square mile. (In comparison, the U.S. average is 74 persons per square mile, which still leaves lot of empty space.) Even the areas populated by livestock and their herders look unspoiled to the eye. The livestock merely cut the grass, and there are no fences separating pastures. The undeveloped transportation and communication systems also result in land remaining pristine. Cement highways and the car exhaust, leaked oil, and ice-melting salt that come with them are almost entirely absent from the country. So are cell phone towers, electrical poles, transformers, and power lines. The terrain is extraordinarily varied, including both the world's northernmost desert, the Gobi, and vast tracts of permanently frozen land, permafrost (Mongolia is the place in the world where permafrost and desert are closest together). There are mountains, lakes, glaciers, rivers, inactive volcanoes, painted deserts, forests, and vast, vast plains of grass called steppes.

Nonetheless, Mongolia's landscape is fragile. The Mongolians, Soviets, and now other foreigners have mined without considering environ-

Overgrazing, devastating weather, and pollution have threatened Mongolia's beautiful environment in the decade since 1990. (AP/Wide World Photos/ Chien-Min Chung)

mental impact. Many of Mongolia's energy sources are very polluting. Hunters and fishermen desperate for cash are decimating certain populations of wildlife, either within or outside the law. As discussed in chapter 6 below, capitalism has encouraged overgrazing of land and overpopulation of livestock. Very cold ecosystems tend to be fragile and easily disrupted. Because Mongolia is still so dependent on the land and its animals for survival, it is important that it safeguard them.

Climate and Conditions

Mongolia borders Siberia and resembles its neighbor in many ways: Half of Mongolia is covered by permafrost. Winters last from early October through April. The final spring frost in regions of Mongolia that do thaw is usually at the end of May; the first autumn frost arrives during the first week of September. This yields a growing season of at most four months. In January, temperatures can drop to –62 degrees Fahrenheit. Even in the summer, temperatures often only reach the 60s.

Neither winter nor summer is gray, however. Mongolia is one of the sunniest countries in the world, averaging 257 cloudless days per year. The South is even sunnier than the North, with 3,200 hours of sunshine a year; the North has 2,600 hours. High atmospheric pressure causes clouds to flee; Asian weather patterns are such that the highest atmospheric pressure system in the Northern Hemisphere forms over Mongolia in the winter. It has 200–500 more hours of sunlight per year than nations at similar latitudes.

As one might expect given all of the sunshine, Mongolia receives little rain- or snowfall. In the north, where precipitation is highest, the land receives only eight to 14 inches a year; in the South, it receives only four to eight inches. By comparison, Missouri—neither particularly wet nor particularly dry by U.S. standards—receives 40 inches of precipitation annually. Drought is common in Mongolia, and, as a result of the dry soil, so are sandstorms. Every year, parts of the Gobi Desert experience some 60 days of sandstorms, concentrated in the spring.

Drought also fuels forest and grassland fires. In July and August 2002, 119 forest fires broke out in Mongolia, affecting the capital and 12 of 18 *aymags*. In Ulaanbaatar alone, fires broke out in eight separate places. By the end of August, almost 20 percent of the country's already small forest reserves (only 8 percent of the country is forested) had burned. Forest fires occur every year, despite the efforts of the government to extinguish them (organizations with more than 50 employees may be mobilized to fight them).

Mongolia is a seismically active country; it has many earthquakes. Because the country is so sparsely populated and has so few large structures that can fall and cause further damage, these quakes do not tend to be particularly destructive to human life. Nonetheless, they are powerful. In the 20th century, Mongolia experienced significant earthquakes in 1905, in Hangai (central Mongolia), and in 1931, 1957, and 1967, in the Gobi-Altai, in southwest Mongolia. The 1905 quake was estimated at magnitude (M) 8.2 to 8.7 on the Richter scale (the hugely destructive San Francisco earthquake of 1906 registered a magnitude of 8.3). The 1957 quake was estimated at 7.9–8.3 M, and resulted in about 20 deaths. The 1967 quake was estimated at 7.5 M, with the largest aftershock at 7.0 M.

Though not as lethal as some, Mongolian earthquakes have been quite disruptive to water flow and movement of nomads and their animals. For example, the fault line moving in the 1905 earthquake is one of the longest active fault lines in the world, at 248 miles. During the 1905 quake, a fissure (similar to a crevice) that was 180 feet deep and more than 30 feet wide opened in the ground. This caused streams, on which vegetation and herd animals are dependent, to change course.

Mongolia can be loosely divided into three geographic regions: the mountains in the West, North, and North-Central; the steppe, in central Mongolia; and the Gobi Desert area, in the South. Each has very different vegetation, wildlife, and topographical features.

Mountains

Mongolia has three major mountain ranges. The highest, the Altai, covers the western-southwestern part of the country. The Hangayn Nuruu covers central and north-central Mongolia. The lowest range, the Hentiyn Nuruu, is in the northeast. Due to its location and its mountains, Mongolia strides three continental divides, mountain ranges from which water flowing down one side goes to one ocean and water flowing down the other side goes to a different collection point. In Mongolia's case, some water is directed from its mountains thousands of miles north to the Arctic Ocean; some goes to the Pacific; and some drains into the Central Asian basin, never reaching any ocean.

Mongolia has some 1,200 rivers, with a total length of 43,400 miles. The main rivers draining into the Arctic are the Selenge and its tributary the Orhon. The Selenge is the main river flowing into Russia's extraordinary Lake Baikal, the oldest (25 million years) and deepest (4,911 feet) lake in the world, containing 20 percent of the world's unfrozen freshwater. (By contrast, the five Great Lakes combined only hold 18 percent.) The major rivers of the Pacific basin are the Onon, on whose banks Genghis Khan grew up, the Ulz, the Herlen, and the Halhyn Gol. The largest river draining into the Central Asian basin is the Hovd. All of the rivers in Mongolia freeze in the winter, most for 140–180 days, or five to six months. The ice is, on average, 30–45 inches thick.

Forty-one species of fish live in the rivers flowing into the Pacific. These include the sturgeon, carp, skin-carp, bullhead, and Mongolian red-feather fish. Twenty-five species populate the Arctic basin rivers.

These include the whitefish, lenok (a type of trout), pike, burbot, and perch. Only five species live in the rivers of the Central Asian basin. The three most common of these are the Mongolian grayling, the Altai mountain dace, and the Siberian stone-loach.

The mountains also hold freshwater in the form of glaciers. Mongolia has hundreds, each relatively small. Most are in the high reaches of the Altai Mountains. Mongolia's largest glaciers are the Potanin, 12 miles long and with an area of about 20 square miles; the Przhevalski, seven miles long and with an area of about 11 square miles; and the Garnet, five miles long. All told, the glaciers cover only about 190 square miles. In comparison, the state of Alaska, similar in area to Mongolia, has 100,000 square miles covered by glaciers. Mongolia's glaciers vary in thickness from about 75 feet to 420 feet.

Vegetation in the mountains and surrounding land consists of cedar and larch (both evergreens), lichen (the perfect reindeer food), moss, birch, low shrubs, and small alpine plants. Some of the flowers are typical of mountain meadows outside Mongolia—gentian, Shasta daisies, and edelweiss—some are exclusive to the region. Of the latter, the sausserea, "sky flower," is particularly venerated. It is reclusive and held to be sacred, growing in the mountains of western Mongolia and reaching its peak in August. Large and brown, it grows only in pairs, known as the "king" and "queen." The head of the flower is heavy and tends to droop, always in the direction of its mate. People believe that the flower can grant wishes, bless love, and heal diseases. They therefore make pilgrimages up into the mountains in search of it. It is forbidden to share its exact location, so the process of finding sausserea can be arduous. To add to the problem, good weather—sunny and calm—is thought to be required. If one wishes to have prayers answered by the sausserea, one should kneel, remove one's hat, place one's arms across one's chest and whisper one's wishes or the name of one's love to the flower. If one needs to pick the flower for medicinal purposes, one should build a tent around the flower and wait for night. The flower should be cut, wrapped in a cloth or scarf, and taken out to be dried only at night. It is believed that if the flower is used for mere decoration, bad luck will befall the user.

The mountains, which are almost unpopulated, teem with wildlife well-adapted to the extremely harsh conditions. Wild sheep, gazelles, ibexes, and snow leopards casually scale nearly sheer, icy walls; ermine and mountain hare live among them. The profusion of birds includes the golden eagle, Altai snowcock, mountain snipe, Himalayan dunnock, rock ptarmigan, polar bunting, rock pigeon, and Brandt's rosy finch. In the nearby forests live marmots, muskrats, squirrels, chipmunks, foxes, steppe foxes, wolves, wild boar, brown bears, antelopes, reindeer, elks, moose, beavers, sables, lynxes, and the glutton (known to North Americans as the wolverine). More birds inhabit the forested and rocky areas, the nutcracker, jay, hazel-hen, and azure-winged magpie among them. Oddly, the cold land is also home to lizards, including the viviparous lizard, the world's most northern species of lizard, the Mongolian toad, and the northern viper. The northern viper is poisonous but deadly only to the young, old, or otherwise frail.

The snow leopard is one of Mongolia's wildlife treasures. Officially listed as endangered by the World Conservation Union, there are only some 4,000–6,000 remaining in the mountains of Central Asia, its habitat. Unlike the others in its animal family, the big cats, the snow leopard is relatively small at only 70–100 lb. and is incapable of the impressive roar that lions and other leopards can make.

The snow leopard prefers to live in craggy areas above the tree line, at 5,000–18,000 feet above sea level. Its body is well adapted to such an environment. Its coat, much sought after by hunters, is patterned irregularly with dark rosettes on a white, cream, or light gray background, which provides for good camouflage against gray rocks. Its tail is extremely long in proportion to its body (they are almost the same length). This helps it to balance on icy, rocky ridges. The tail also provides warmth, as it can be wrapped around the body and across the face like a muffler.

The snow leopard preys on blue sheep, ibexes, marmots, argalis, tahrs, other wild goats and sheep, hares, birds, and domestic livestock. It usually hunts alone, lying in wait for its prey and then leaping upon it from a distance of up to 45 feet. It is capable of bringing down an animal three times its size. It is equipped with a rough tongue to remove fur and skin from its kill and can feed for many days upon a carcass, because there are few animals to disturb it and the freezing weather prevents decomposition. To survive, it needs to bring down 20–30 blue sheep a year, or their equivalent in other animals.

The snow leopard is severely threatened by hunters, a decline in the population of the animals it preys on, and encroachment by humans upon its habitat. Despite the legal protection of the 1973 Convention on International Trade in Endangered Species of Wild Flora and Fauna, demand for its bones (for Chinese medicine) and fur encourages hunting. Mongolian herdsmen, often so poor that the loss of a single animal is devastating, sometimes shoot the snow leopard to protect their flocks. Programs have started that give such herdspeople food or clothing in return for not killing the leopards. One of the reasons that snow leopards find themselves near domestic livestock is destruction of their preferred, higher habitat due to mining or hunting. Mongolia is attempting to improve enforcement of its environmental laws and protected reserves.

Steppe

Steppe is a word of Russian origin for a semi-arid, grassy, lightly wooded plain. Although there are areas of North America that would probably meet this definition, the word is usually reserved for lands in Eurasia. The steppe fostered Mongolia's growth as a nation. It is where its earliest people domesticated the yak, the camel, the horse, and other animals now used as livestock; where Mongolians learned the horse-riding skills that allowed them to reach and conquer parts of Europe when it was still in the Dark Ages; where, despite the rough weather, many Mongolians still feel most at home. The steppe has never been fenced or subdivided in any way; the few roads across it are little more than tire tracks. Even under capitalism, it seems unlikely that it will be chopped up into privately held pieces any time soon.

The steppe is low on trees, but richly carpeted with grasses, some of which if left uneaten grow as high as a person. The dominant plants include sandy steppe feather-grass, serpentine feather-grass, sage brush feather-grass, and feather-grass caragana. In addition to domestic livestock, the steppe is home to the saiga antelope, jerba rodent, marmot, yak, gopher, dog fox, wild cat, and pole cat. Common birds include the crane, the great bustard, the steppe falcon, the steppe eagle, the Mongolian lark, the dancing wheatear, and the tawny pipit. The Mongolian lizard also survives on the steppe.

The Mongolian steppe is also one of the only places in the world that harbors wild horses. Known to Westerners as the Przewalski horse, to Mongolians as *takhi* (meaning "spirit"), these animals once roamed the steppe in herds, much as buffalo roamed the American West. Not merely a wild version of the domesticated horse, *takhi* are significantly different in genetic structure and unique in appearance. Their bodies have evolved to be camouflaged on the steppe. In winter, *takhis'* white bellies blend in with the snow; their backs are light tan. In summer, their hair turns darker. They have no forelock, and their legs have zebra-like stripes.

Like buffalo, *takhi* populations were decimated by hunting and encroachment on their habitat by humans. *Takhi* became extinct in Mongolia as of 1969. Some were preserved in captivity, bred there, and 32 were reintroduced into Mongolia in 1992 on a reserve west of Ulaanbaatar. The reserve includes three enclosed areas where the horses gradually get used to their new freedom for a few years. They are then released into the wild in "harems" made up of several females and one male. There are now more than 200 *takhi* living in Mongolia. The government protects those in the area of the reserve by hiring local herdsmen, who might otherwise be tempted to hunt the *takhi*, as rangers or as workers at the park's cheese factory.

Lakes

Mingled throughout Mongolia's mountains, forests, valleys, and steppe are nearly 4,000 lakes. Most are small; 95 percent are less than two square miles. The remaining 5 percent are very large, however, comprising 6,150 square miles of surface area. Most (80 percent) are freshwater, but some are slightly salty. Some lakes formed when tectonic plate—large pieces of the Earth's crust—boundaries left a fissure following an earthquake. Some arose from water filling a volcanic crater. Many are fed by runoff from either former or current glaciers and have an unearthly blue-green hue. Hovsgol, the second largest and deepest lake in Mongolia, is fed by more than 90 rivers. It is extremely pure and transparent (visibility goes down 48 to 75 feet), a beneficiary of its isolation from sources of pollution. The largest lake in Mongolia, Uvs Nuur, is at lower altitude and is saline, with a salt content of about 11–12 percent. This makes it about one-third as salty as the ocean.

The lakes and other water sources and the territory surrounding them are a focal point of the many migrations that occur across Mongolia every year. Birds are the most skilled migrants; almost all of the birds that summer in the Arctic travel to the Indian and Pacific Oceans via Mongolia for the winter. Many birds winter elsewhere but summer in Mongolia, including the mountain goose, swan goose, hooper swan, and European teal. Moreover, some birds summer in the Arctic but find Mongolian winters mild enough to winter in; these include the snowy owl and snow bunting.

Fish also migrate within Mongolia's lakes and river system. The Baikal sturgeon covers almost 200 miles in its migrations to reproduce in the Selenge and Orhon Rivers. The Amur sheat-fish and Amur carp make their way from the Selenge River to Uvs Nuur Lake. Taimen leave the rivers for the lakes in the winter. Among mammals, the Mongolian antelope used to migrate nearly 1,000 miles from the southeast to Uvs Nuur and the Orhon River, but this has recently stopped, perhaps because of habitat changes.

Gobi Desert

The Gobi has Mongolia's harshest climate, experiencing great cold in the winter, heat in the summer, lack of water year-round, and frequent sandstorms. The desert in some parts is devoid of vegetation and covered with sand dunes. Most of it, however, has some scrubby vegetation, like saxual, salt wort, sagebrush, nitre, and ephedran, a dry, low pine that contains the powerful stimulant ephedra. Animals live off these and each other; Gobi inhabitants include the wild ass, wild camel, cashmere goat, Gobi bear, Gobi argali sheep, ibex, black-tailed gazelle, Mongolian hamster and other rodents, marbled polecat, and red wolf. Lizards, with their water-protective skin, are well adapted to the climate. These include the squeaky gecko and Przewalski gecko in sandy/rocky areas and the gay toad and agamas in areas known as the Farewell Rocks and Stacks.

Some birds also make their home in the Gobi: the pallass sand grouse, the Mongolian desert jay, and the Mongolian desert finch among them. The Houbara bustard, a shy bird with a flat breast and spiky head, is able to extract metabolic water from the insects and seeds it eats. The cinerous vulture, with a wingspan of 8–9.5 feet and at 18 pounds weighing more than a small dog, is able to fly above the hottest air masses. The Henderson's ground jay, a roadrunner-type bird, is also adapted to hot climates.

Of the desert's inhabitants, the Gobi bear is perhaps the most vulnerable. Estimates of its remaining numbers on Earth range from under 20 to about 30. The Gobi bear, known as *mazaalai* in Mongolian, is a largely vegetarian bear that is smaller than its forest-dwelling relatives. Because it lives in the inhospitable Gobi, its diet is limited to the small number of plants and animals available there. It lives on leaves, berries, grass roots, and the occasional lizard or mouse. It does not have the luxury of rejecting as a meal even insects like grasshoppers or beetles. A female bear may weigh only 220 pounds or so.

The Gobi bear's survival is threatened by human and livestock activities such as overgrazing and pumping well water, which turns already dry land into true, infertile desert. Life for a large animal with a substantial need of food and water is already precarious in a desert environment, without these problems.

FOSSILS

The Gobi was not always inhospitable. Like parts of Montana, Wyoming, and the western United States, where dinosaur fossils are also plentiful, Mongolia, cold and dry today, once (100 million–65 million years ago) had warm, wet oases. The mild, humid environment of the oases was friendly to dinosaurs, while the later dry climate has preserved their remains well. Beginning in the 1920s, the Mongolian Gobi has been the site of extraordinary fossil finds by paleontologists.

An American scientist, Roy Chapman Andrews (1884–1960), discovered the first fossil dinosaur eggs ever found (scientists had not been sure that dinosaurs laid eggs) in the Gobi Desert. Andrews also discovered *Protoceratops andrewsi* (named after him), velociraptors, and an oviraptor ("egg stealer") fossilized in the act of trying to steal another dinosaur's eggs. Many of the dinosaurs found fossilized appear to have been killed by sudden sandstorms (which helped to preserve them). One oviraptor was found in the act of trying to protect its nest from such sands. Fossils of a protoceratops and a velociraptor were found fossilized in the act of combat, with the velociraptor's claws in the protoceratops's stomach and the protoceratops biting the velociraptor's arm.

Other finds include the *Pachycephalosaurs slegoceras*, which used its extra-bony skull as a battering ram; the *Elotherium*, with a periscope-style nose permitting it to breathe while the rest of its body was submerged; and the *Therizinosaurus*, with claws almost two feet long; and *Tarbosaurus*, a *Tyrannosaurus rex*–like creature (*T. Rex* is North American) with six-inch-long teeth. Dinosaurs were reptiles; fossils of the largest land mammal thought to have lived also have been found in the Gobi. Rhinoceros-like in appearance, they were four times as large as modern-day elephants.

Resources, Problems, and Solutions

Aside from sustaining the nomadic way of life, Mongolia's land provides it with sources of minerals, energy, exports, and recreation. Each of these, however, in addition to the herding lifestyle, presents its own challenges to the land.

MINERALS

Mongolia's wealth of resources above ground is echoed below, where vast reserves of minerals are being explored and exploited. Mongolia has already been discovered to be rich in gold, coal, copper, molybdenum, tungsten, and fluorspar (all used in metal processing/strengthening); tin, nickel, zinc, phosphates (used as fertilizers); and salt. Although international prospecting is still in its infancy, Mongolia has also been discovered to have iron, manganese (used in steel and iron production), titanium (most used to make titanium white paint), vanadium (used in strengthening metals for machines such as cars and jets), cobalt, lead, silver, platinum, and a variety of rare-earth elements.

Such resources present an important source of revenue for the country in the future, but mining and use of minerals also come at a heavy environmental price. Mining can strip the countryside and create runoff of toxic materials into lakes, rivers, and soil. Many of Mongolia's main rivers—the Selenge, Orkhon, Yeruu, Kharaa, and Tuul—have already become quite polluted by mining operations. Current environmental laws in the country do not require restoration of land after mining ceases. The Tuul, Ulaanbaatar's main source of drinking water, has also been polluted by the more than 80 leather-processing plants in its drainage area. The plants also have caused a drop in the water level of the Tuul by siphoning off water and then draining it away from the Tuul. A new environmental organization, Save the Tuul, is trying to change these practices. Coal-burning has created serious air pollution problems in Ulaanbaatar. And until recently, vehicles were allowed to use frozen lakes as highways in the winter, contaminating the lakes with oil.

RECREATION

Threats to Mongolia's environment also come from hunting, fishing, and otherwise capturing wildlife, although in moderation these are all sustainable activities.

Fishing

Fishing has never been a popular sport in Mongolia because Mongolians do not enjoy fish. Through the end of the Communist era, therefore, Mongolia's huge fish population was largely left to grow and live undisturbed. Since the country was opened to foreigners in the early 1990s, it, like Siberia, has been revealed to be a fishing paradise.

The largest fish inhabiting Mongolia's waters is the taimen or Hucho taimen, reaching as much as 80 pounds and six feet in length (it averages two to three feet). The taimen is a distant cousin of the Atlantic salmon. More popular, however, is the Durkhat Whitefish, available only in the lakes of Darkhat Valley in extreme north-central Mongolia. The whitefish averages about two feet in length and weighs eight pounds but is almost boneless and tender. Also popular are lenok, grayling, and pike.

Though Mongolians are not enthusiastic fishermen, they have developed some traditional fishing methods. One is spiking, which involves (naturally) sitting on a horse in the middle of a river and using a large spoon-like device to catch the fish. They also use the familiar hook on a rope. Less traditional creative methods have also occurred to Mongolians. When fishing for a taimen, Mongolians will tempt its gigantic appetite (for a fish) with a mouse or ground squirrel tossed into the water. One fisherman is known to have ripped the arms and legs off his child's teddy bear and placed hooks in it. In desperation, Mongolians will also attempt to net fish with shirts.

If the fishing boom continues, many are concerned about the future of fish populations. The Soviets did do some damage during their occupation, using dynamite and other illegal means of catching fish, but many believe that present methods could far exceed the Soviets' in damage. Companies exporting fish to China and Russia have already set up large operations at Buir Nuur Lake and the Darkhat Lakes valley. It is difficult for Mongolians to decline the economic boost such operations bring, especially when they do not have much use for the resource.

Hunting

Hunting is not an extremely popular sport in Mongolia, perhaps because living among animals is part of daily life for many Mongolians. One ethnic group in western Mongolia, however, the Kazakhs, are well known for their exotic style of hunting. Their partner in their method, which goes back 2,000 years, is the female golden eagle. The female is one-third heavier than the male golden eagle and much more aggressive. Kazakhs capture wild eagles when they are young. They wash them, feed them well, and "break" them by tying them to a wooden block. When the eagle tries to fly away, it has to carry the wooden block with it. Not strong enough to do so, it falls to the ground repeatedly. After two days it is completely fatigued and frustrated and disposed to training. During training, the heavy block is removed, but the eagle is leashed to a pole called a *tugir*. It is taught to go after animal skins.

When the bird is trained, the Kazakhs take it hunting, but only in November and December when the pelts of prey are at their thickest. A Kazakh will ride on horseback with a greyhound dog (also used for hunting) draped across the saddle and a golden eagle on the wrist. A leather glove is worn to protect the skin from the eagle's sharp talons. The eagle is hooded when not on the hunt. Eagles capture marmots, small foxes, and wolves, and then release them to the hunter, who clubs the animals to death and rewards the eagle with a cut of the meat. An eagle can live and hunt for about 30 years, but most hunters release the birds back into the wild after 10 years.

Even untrained to follow human commands, Mongolian birds of prey are extremely valuable. Corruption in the Mongolian government is to blame for smuggling in the rare Mongolian falcon. The birds are prized by the oil magnates of the Middle East. Falcon breeding farms, another source of the birds, produce much poorer hunters. Only one in 10 farm-raised birds can match the hunting skills the Mongolian falcons come by naturally. In a legal transaction, the United Arab Emirates, Saudi Arabia, and Kuwait pledged $3 million in development funds in exchange for 80 Mongolian falcons. The birds were flown out on a special plane equipped with roosts where there normally are seats.

As many or far more wild birds leave the country illegally, making Mongolia one of the centers of the world in the illegal trade of rare birds. Customers on the illegal market are willing to pay as much as $200,000 for the best birds. In 1997, Mongolian customs officials prevented 26 instances of illegal smuggling. One instance involved the discovery of 14 hidden birds just prior to takeoff of the plane they were being smuggled on. An American falcon expert estimates that $40 million worth of smuggled birds leave the country every year.

Threats to Mongolia's wildlife also come from hunters looking for valuable furs like that of the lynx and snow leopard, and those eager to satisfy the unusual demands of Mongolia's populous neighbor, China. Powdered argali sheep horns, boiled Gobi bear gall bladders, musk deer glands, and snow leopard bones are all in demand by the Chinese for traditional medicines and other uses. In addition, the overgrazing of domestic livestock interferes with necessary habitat.

In response, the Mongolian government has increased its efforts to preserve habitats for animals. There are currently some 50 protected areas, representing about 13 percent of the country's territory. The Ministry of Nature and Environment is aiming eventually for protection of 30 percent of the country's land, which would create the largest park system in the world. A lack of money for protection and enforcement of environmental regulations is a serious obstacle to true conservation, however.

NOTES

p. 68 "It is reclusive . . ." Ch. Uuganbayar, "Sausserea—The Rare Flower of Love, Wishes and Hope," in *Ger Magazine*, Issue 3, January, 2000. Available on-line. URL: http://www.un-mongolia.mn/archives/ger-mag/.

p. 68 "People believe . . ." *Ibid.*

p. 70 "To survive . . ." *"Pantheria uncia*—The Snow Leopard," on "A Leap of Leopards." Available on-line. URL: http://www.geocities.com/RainForest/Andes/ 4613/sl/sleopard.htm. Updated November 21, 1998.

p. 71 "There are now more than . . ." "Takhi (the Mongolian wild horse)," on "Mongolia" website. Available on-line. URL: http://www.halcyon.com/ mongolia/Takhi.html. Updated December 18, 1995.

p. 71 "The government protects . . ." Mayhew, *Mongolia*, p. 183.

p. 72 "Among mammals . . ." Consulate of Mongolia, "Fauna." Available on-line. URL: http://www.mongolia.org.hk/country_info-1-09.htm. Site updated January 30, 2002.

p. 75 "Current environmental laws . . ." "Mongolian Commentator Warns on Pollution from Gold Mining," in BBC *Monitoring International Reports*, May 21, 2002.

p. 75 "The plants also have caused . . ." "Water Levels of Mongolia's River Tuul Sinking," in BBC *Monitoring International Reports*, May 15, 2002.

p. 77 "An American falcon expert . . ." "Falcon Hunting Season," in *Mongolia Today*, Issue 2. Available on-line. URL: http://www.mongoliatoday.com/ issue/2/falcon_trade_1.html. Posted 1999–2002.

p. 77 "Powdered argali . . ." Mayhew, *Mongolia*, p. 42.

p. 77 "There are currently some 50 . . ." Mayhew, *Mongolia*, p. 29.

6

THE HERDING LIFE

There is a saying that Mongolia's land was designed by God for nomadic herding. About half of Mongolians participate in the herding economy, Mongolia's traditional means of subsistence. However, herding is more than a job to Mongolians. It involves a deep, spiritual relationship with animals; vigilant observation of the land and weather; and an ability to make a home without accumulating a large number of heavy possessions that would hamper movement. It also requires an ability to be happy without most of the sources of entertainment people in cities enjoy: other people, markets, sporting events, street life, movies, and multiple television channels, among others. In exchange for these sacrifices (which they do not view as such), herders benefit from a deep connection to Mongolia's past and have an opportunity to preserve its customs.

The environment, for herders, is not without change, however. Wolves, which the Communists targeted for extermination, have staged a comeback and are stealing livestock. Since the transition to a market economy in Mongolia and Russia, desperate Russians have begun raiding herding camps in northern Mongolia to steal animals for food. Larger changes in the environment and the herding economy since privatization, combined with bad weather, have produced a natural disaster known as *dzud* for several years now. It has brought tragedy to many herders' lives. It seems likely that the effect of the livestock predators and *dzud* will abate as herders come together in communities and adjust to the market economy, but this will take some work.

The Ger

The *ger* is a round, flexible, transportable, seasonally adaptable, single-room tent that has been the traditional Mongolian home for centuries. Although *ger* have pitched roofs, from a distance they can look like marshmallows scattered on green pastures. About half of all Mongolians still live in a *ger*. It is the home of nomadic farmers, and there are even many *ger* districts within towns and Ulaanbaatar. Some city *ger* are factory-made of aluminum or are attached to generators to provide electricity. Some are also designed not to be moved often and are surrounded by fences and assigned a number so they can receive mail and other services. Most *ger*, however, are still the traditional cylindrical tents, light enough to be transported by four camels but sturdy enough to withstand winds and temperatures in the dozens of degrees below zero on the steppe.

The structure of the *ger* is composed of essentially four parts: the floor, the walls, the door, and the roof. In erecting the *ger* at a new location, the floor is laid first. Then the walls are erected. Ger walls (*qana*) are accordion-like lattices that can be compacted for transportation or stretched out to form curved walls. The accordion structure is made of wood slats tied together with rawhide. The number of *qana* units determines the circumference of the structure and, therefore, the size of the *ger*. A common herder may have a *ger* of four units. A wealthier herder may have six to eight. Before the Communist era, the "palace" *ger* of religious leaders or nobles had 10–12 units. To complete the sides of the *ger*, the door is fit into place. For religious reasons (see chapter 6) it always faces south.

Next, two wooden posts are fit into the center of the floor. On top of them is placed a small wooden wheel that will form the opening in the roof to let out smoke and let in light and air. Then, long orange poles are inserted into holes in the wheel on one end and the top of the walls on the other end. The result resembles another wheel, which forms the ceiling of the *ger*. The poles are orange to resemble the Sun and for good luck.

This structure must be covered in order to protect it from sun, wind, and cold. The most important element of this covering is felt. Felt is used not only for *ger* but for rugs, stockings, saddles, and so forth, and its production is a traditional Mongolian art. Each household makes its own felt. It is done in the autumn, and most members of the household participate in the undertaking.

Felt consists of specially treated wool and holds together because the wool fibers have little barbs that lock together when processed. To make felt, wool (taken directly from sheep) is first beaten to loosen the fibers. Then, Mongolians take a piece of old felt, called the "mother felt." It is placed on the ground and moistened. A layer of new sheep's wool is placed on top of it, wetted again. Two more layers of new wool are then added, each moistened in turn. Grass is placed on top, and then the entire bundle is rolled up (the grass prevents the wool from forming a huge mass). This roll is wrapped in a wet ox hide and fastened with leather straps. Once again, it is thoroughly wetted, with water poured inside each end of the roll. The roll is tied with a long leather rope, and two riders on horseback take each end and pull it in opposite directions, squeezing out the water and pressing the wool firmly into place. Then the package is unrolled and people proclaim the birth of "sweet daughter" felt. The entire process is then repeated using the daughter felt as the starter.

When used for the covering of a *ger*, felt is not dyed. It is wrapped around and outside the walls, covers the roof, and is used for the flap that covers the smokehole when it is not in use. In hot weather, the portion of the wall covering low to the ground can be rolled up or removed to allow air to flow through the *ger*. Otherwise, the felt is tied down over the *ger* with horsehair ropes. To help preserve the felt and to protect against water, the felt may be treated either with tallow (animal fat) or covered with cotton canvas. The felt and canvas are not dyed, and so *gers* appear white or cream-colored on the outside.

Inside the *ger*, a brick or metal stove sits in the center. This is used for heat as well as cooking in the winter. Across from the *ger*'s door sits a marriage bed, which is symbolic and not used for sleeping. It holds quilts, clothing, and pillows and may be used for seating. In front of the bed, also facing the door, is a place of honor for guests. Beds for sleeping may be curtained and are placed at the sides of the *ger*. Men's items are set on the left side of the *ger* in order to be protected by the sky god (see chapter 7, under "Religion"). These include tools, a saddle, and a leather bag for *airag*, the popular drink of fermented mare's milk. Women's items are set on the right. These include kitchen items. Around the sides of the *ger* there are usually stools, brightly painted chests, mirrors, and, perhaps, photographs or religious pictures. The floor is covered with rugs.

Herders benefit from Mongolia's ever-present sunshine in more ways than one.
(AP/Wide World Photos/Greg Baker)

These days, *ger* also have some modern conveniences. Most herders have transistor radios, used to receive up-to-date weather reports. Many households also have a TV, a sewing machine, and a bicycle, motorcycle, or truck.

The Nomadic Lifestyle

Outside the *ger*'s walls, the Mongolian herding lifestyle is based upon a relationship among people; the "five snouts," or five principal animals; and the land. The land is in large part what has dictated the lifestyle: the altitude is high, the growing season is short, and places that provide good grazing in the summer are often not sufficiently protected from winter winds and snows. The grass is only so plentiful in any given place, but the land as a whole is vast. Horses, camels, cattle (including yaks), sheep and goats, the five snouts, are all native to the region, accustomed to grazing over wide stretches of land. Over time, the Mongolians have become so accustomed to their nomadic lifestyle that many disdain forms of work that cannot be done on horseback, such as growing crops. They are also prejudiced against food that does not come from the five snouts. For example, although Mongolia's rivers teem with fish, Mongolians mostly ignore them. They also reject vegetables, believing that "meat is for men, leaves are for animals." They have elevated the five snouts to national symbols and objects of love, telling folktales about them and representing them on the national seal.

The basic unit of nomadic Mongolian life is the herding camp, or *khot ail*, generally composed of two to 12 households. Somewhat surprisingly, Mongolians do not tend to camp or travel with their extended families, although some families within a *khot ail* may be related by blood or marriage. The *khot ail* tend to be larger in fertile areas and smaller in areas of poorer land. The households within the *khot ail* cooperate on herding, cutting the animals' wool and hair for use, making felt, making hay, and moving camp. Groups of *khot ails* may join forces to look for lost animals and to coordinate use of land. A *khot ail* is led by the most experienced male herder. The composition of a *khot ail* is not fixed for life. A household may be part of one *khot ail* one year, part of a different one the next.

The camp moves at least once a year, from winter camp to summer grazing land. Some camps move as often as once a month in search of better grassland. These movements have never been rigidly fixed, but there are patterns for every camp. Historically, Mongols have not usually recognized private ownership of specific parcels of land. They have, however, recognized claims to use particular areas in the country, such as springs, streambanks near good grazing land, or protected winter camp sites. There was some mutual recognition that every camp needed access to at least some of the above for some of the year, but there also could be conflict over particular locations at particular times. Even so, however, if natural disasters fell upon particular areas, neighboring families would allow the herdsmen to temporarily change locations.

The summer is the time for grazing. Camels are allowed to stray as much as 30 miles from camp and may be left alone for months on end. Fall is the time to prepare for winter, which includes felt making, slaughtering animals, and drying meat to last through winter. Fall is the only time Mongols slaughter large numbers of animals. They kill the ones that seem too weak to survive the winter in order to provide themselves with food, since sheep and horses do not produce milk in the winter. In

October, at the latest, the group moves to its winter camp. The winter camp location is the most fixed. To withstand the harsh winters, groups usually pick an area somewhat protected from wind and blowing snow. Mongolians traditionally kept permanent stone shelters for the animals, which survived on dried grass throughout the winter. They also built a fence around *ger* to keep out some of the blowing and drifting snow. During the Communist era, the government improved these shelters and worked to provide reliable fodder for the animals. Now, some winter camps have portable power generators to provide electricity. In the spring, the group forms a caravan led by women and moves once again.

A nomadic family's typical day involves herding and care of horses by the men and care of sheep and goats and performance of various household tasks by women. It is normal for a man to spend 10 hours a day either on horseback or in a motorcycle or jeep. In the morning, he drives the herd out to pasture, spends the day making sure the animals do not stray too far, and brings the animals back at night for watering and milking. To control animals, the men use long, 25–30-foot poles with rawhide rope nooses on the end. The women cook, milk camels and goats, make yogurt or cheese, clean, sew, and gather dried dung for fuel.

The Five Snouts

The horse is by far the most important—and beloved—of the five snouts. There are approximately the same number of horses in Mongolia as there are people—well over 2 million. Horses are not usually used for meat but for riding and milk. Mongolian horses are on the short side, with long and thick hair, tail, and mane. They are known for being fast, powerful, and lively. Mongolians use different kinds of horses for different purposes and seasons. In the winter, they tend to ride horses with a particularly thick hide and coat, firm hooves, and stout legs. Summer mounts should have thinner hides and hair, not be overworked, and not be overly wild. Horses used for when the herdsman wants to lasso other animals should be of average weight, steady, with a short body and the ability to start and stop quickly to keep up with the other animals' movements.

The virtues of horses are extolled by Mongolia's language, music, and literature. The Mongolian language has more than 300 terms used to describe horses by color, body type, identifying marks, and so forth. *Mori* is the word for a gelding, a male horse. *Xiimori*, a flying magical horse, means "healthy." *Morisaitai* means "lucky" or "someone who owns a good horse." Mongols have more songs about the love of horses than about the love of women, and in Mongolian epics the horse is often the hero's best adviser and is able to predict future events.

The second snout, camels, were domesticated more than 3,000 years ago in Mongolia. Camels are extremely well adapted for life in a cold, dry, rugged climate. They are primarily used in the part of Mongolia nearest to and containing the Gobi Desert. About two-thirds of the camels in Mongolia, or 235,000 animals, live in this area. They have no trouble being worked even in the coldest winter temperatures. They can go a month without food and a week without water and will settle for scrubby vegetation and salty water when they can get it. In the *dzuds* (see page 92) of the last several years, camels have survived where goats and sheep quickly died. Drooping humps are a sign of thirst, hunger, or otherwise poor health. If parched, a camel can drink 50 gallons of water in a day. Since water in the Gobi must usually be drawn by hand from wells, it can take several hours to water a herd. Other difficulties in dealing with camels somewhat offset the advantage of their minimal dietary requirements. If a baby camel is attacked by a wolf, its owner must tie its legs up, wrestle it to the ground, sew up the wound, and then rub pitch (a tar-like substance) on it, all the while keeping the large, concerned mother at bay. Camels are also more difficult to milk than cows. A baby camel must be allowed to suck first to get the mother's milk going.

Camels are used for their milk, meat, hair, hide, and for transportation of heavy items, like *ger*. Historically, they had more of an important and ceremonial role than they do now. Camels were once, in caravans, the main means of transporting items for trade across wide expanses, such as from Asia to Europe. They still carry 30 percent of the cargo in the Gobi. At one time, a white camel was used to bring a bride from her parents' to her new home. The two-humped Bactrian camel is more commonly used than the one-hump. Both can carry 400–500 pounds of goods on their back, but two-humped camels are faster. "Fast" for a fully loaded camel is about three miles an hour, or the pace of a relatively speedy adult human. Without a load on its back, a camel can outrun a horse. In addition to being hardy pack animals, camels provide other resources amply. Each

Transportation in the Gobi has changed little since the early 20th century.
(Courtesy Library of Congress)

one provides up to 11 pounds of hair every year, 150 gallons of milk, and more than 500 pounds of dung (used for fuel).

Camels are less numerous than horses in Mongolia, a reflection of their diminished importance. There is approximately one camel for every six Mongolians. Since the transition to capitalism, however, the camel population has been suffering. To satisfy their industry's requirement of producing a certain poundage of meat, farmers were killing camels since they are so much heavier than smaller animals, even though the meat is less desirable. In 1994, the government was forced to ban the killing of camels temporarily to halt the decline in their number.

The third snout, cattle, includes yaks and Mongolian cattle. Yaks are an extremely furry relative of the cow, well adapted to life in a harsh climate. They are sure-footed and move easily in mountainous terrain.

Compared to ordinary cattle, they have larger lungs and three times as many blood cells, allowing them to carry oxygen in their bodies at altitudes where oxygen is in short supply. Their heavy coats and small number of sweat glands are designed to withstand extreme cold. Yaks find summer in low Mongolian elevations uncomfortable and enjoy bathing in nearly frozen rivers and lakes and eating snow for water. Mongolian cattle are a special breed also adapted to temperature extremes. There are one and a half times as many cattle in Mongolia as there are people.

Whereas mare's (horse's) milk is used for *airag,* cow's milk is used for drinks as well as a variety of cheeses, creams, and desserts (see "Diet," page 88). Dung for fuel is another important cattle by-product, as are meat and hides. Cowhide is used for ropes, saddles, and boots. Cow horns are used to make the Mongolian bow.

Sheep, the fourth snout, come in different breeds, but all are fat-tailed. These sheep literally have a tail weighing up to 20 pounds made up entirely of fat. The tail is a delicacy and is presented to guests. Sheep produce wool, milk, mutton, and sheepskin, and their blood and intestines are used in sausage. Of the five snouts, sheep are the most numerous. There are approximately six times as many sheep in Mongolia as there are people.

Nomads are extremely comfortable around animals, riding and herding animals much larger than they are. (AP/Wide World Photos/Ng Han Guan)

Goats are the least important of the five snouts, once kept only by very poor people. Even now, goat meat is unpopular, although goat's milk is used for cheeses. Goats' most important products are angora and cashmere wool, both of which are in great demand as exports. Cashmere, a luxury fiber selling for $30–$40 per pound, is the combed-out underdown of almost any species of goat. Each goat, however, only produces a few pounds of the hair per year. Mongolia provides about 20 percent of the world's supply. Goats are well suited to the Mongolian climate and land, as they are able to graze in dry or remote areas inaccessible to cattle. As a result, they are extremely numerous in Mongolia, with a population approximately four times greater than the human one.

In addition to the herding animals, most Mongolian families keep a very fierce dog to guard the *ger* and herd from wolves or other unfriendly visitors. When a friendly stranger approaches a camp, he or she calls out from a distance so that the families will restrain their dogs. It is generally the children's task to come out and hold the dogs down by sitting on their heads. This allows the visitor to enter the *ger* unharmed. Many different breeds of dogs perform this function, but a special Mongolian one is the *bankhar*. It is a large, dark dog with thick fur and a bushy, curly tail. Mongolians call them "four eyes" because of the white spots they have above each eye. Domestic cats, perhaps because they are less useful, are uncommon in Mongolia.

Diet

From the five snouts, Mongolians get almost all of their food (the diet in the cities and towns is often similar to that of herders). Mongolian food, therefore, essentially consists of meat, dairy products, and a few grains prepared in a limited number of ways.

Meat is eaten either fresh or, very frequently, dried. The Mongolians treat fresh meat delicately, never using large axes or saws to cut the carcass. When preparing fresh meat, they usually boil it on the bone, in large pieces. Meat may also be roasted, to prepare a dish called *boodog*. To make *boodog*, an entire animal—a goat or preferably a marmot (rodent)—is slowly roasted from the inside out by filling the skinned carcass with hot rocks, sealing it, and then putting the carcass on the fire or roasting it with a blowtorch.

Cuts of meat are distributed according to status. A guest of honor, for example, receives the saddle of mutton, which he or she then cuts into long, thin slices to distribute to people he or she favors. Lower-status guests receive a mere shoulder-blade of the animal, with two pairs of ribs and part of a leg.

Most meat is eaten dried rather than fresh, however. Mongolians do most of their slaughtering in the late fall, drying the meat so that it will last through the winter. Since animals do not give milk in the winter, meat is the main source of protein then. One cow and seven to eight sheep, or their equivalent, will get a family of five through the winter. In place of beef, herders in the Gobi will preserve camel meat. Mountain herders may kill a yak or goats.

Herders cut the fresh meat into long, inch-thick, and several-inch-wide strips. They hang them on a rope inside the *ger* but near the smoke hole, which is airy. The meat's moisture all evaporates within a month, leaving hard, brown sticks with the texture of wood. The meat shrinks so much that all the meat from an entire cow could fit inside its stomach when dried.

The dried meat, or *borts*, is broken up and stored in a canvas bag that allows air to circulate, so the meat will stay dry. *Borts* may be stored this way for months to years. When herders wish to eat some meat, they add the borts to boiling water. The meat expands in size by two and a half times when placed in water. *Borts* is an ideal food for nomads.

Dairy products provide Mongolians sustenance on a day-to-day, year-round basis. Mongolians produce a variety of different-tasting dairy products from the milk of the five snouts. *Orom* is the cream that rises to the top of boiled milk. *Aarul* are dried cheese curds that Mongolians bake and store on top of *ger* in the summer. *Eetsgii* is another dried cheese. *Tarag* is a sour yogurt. *Shar tos* is a butter formed from melting *aarul* and *orom*. *Tsagaan tos* is boiled *orom* mixed with flour, fruit, or *eetsgii*. Sour varieties of these dairy products are considered good for cleansing the stomach. Consumption of all of these dairy products pales in comparison to the national consumption of *airag*, however.

Airag is a mildly alcoholic drink made of fermented mare's milk. It is made throughout the summer, when mares are producing milk. Herdsmen milk a mare every several hours for a total of six or so times a day. This yields one and a half to two quarts of milk per day, with some left over for the mare's young. Mongolians consume so much *airag* that at this rate of a horse's milk production, a family needs to have at least 12 mares to produce enough milk.

To make *airag*, the fresh milk is mixed with yeast and left in a bag made of hide. To produce the best *airag*, the mixture must be stirred extremely frequently—ideally, some 1,000 times a day. Guests are, therefore, expected to help by whirling the bag. The best *airag* reputedly comes from the middle Gobi Desert, an area called the "Land of *Airag* and Long Songs." The desert grasses eaten by the horses in the area give the milk a unique flavor. Arkhangai province is also known for its *airag*, but here the good taste is attributed to the beauty of the landscape and the beauty of the young milk maidens.

Freshly made *airag* is mild, but if kept long enough, acidity, sourness, and alcohol content increase. Old *airag* may be as alcoholic as wine. It is generally served warm, and, again, a guest of honor receives special treatment when it is served. His or her share will be put in a silver cup placed on a blue silk scarf. After receiving the cup, the guest dips his or her fingers in the *airag* and flicks some three times into the air to bless the sky, soil, and the hearth of the hosts.

Dangers

This peaceful nomadic lifestyle has been threatened since the transition to democracy and capitalism. Larger numbers of animal predators, new human predators, and even the land and climate themselves have decimated herds.

WOLVES

Wolves have always been a danger to herders, as docile livestock are easy prey for the smart, organized, and fast canines. One of V. I. Lenin's promises to those considering revolution was that if the Communists took over, they would kill every last wolf. The Communists tried hard to make good on that promise in Mongolia, establishing two national wolf hunting weeks, one in March and one in December. Anyone who could present the ears of a dead wolf received a sheep and some felt. In May, the government encouraged people to seek out wolf lairs and kill the young cubs. When an area believed it had eradicated all of its wolves, the local government would declare a public holiday. Five thousand to 10,000 wolves were killed annually.

When communism fell, wolf hunting became less organized, and the number of wolves has multiplied. Wolves are believed to be responsible for killing 15,000 head of livestock a year (in addition to killing antelope, wild boar, marmots, and other animals Mongolians value). Hunting wolves has become less a duty that everyone takes on and more a pastime of the newly rich capitalist class. They drive through the countryside in fancy jeeps, attempting to shoot wolves through the windows with high-powered rifles, which is illegal but not actually punished. Herdsmen say, however, that few wolves are killed this way, so the wolf population remains significant.

HUSTLERS

Mongolia now has good relations with the governments of its massive neighbors, China and Russia. Moscow and Beijing, however, are too distant to always succeed in moderating the behavior of their citizens living along Mongolia's borders. Tuva, an independent Russian republic across Mongolia's northern border, is a source of particular friction. During the Communist era, Mongolia exported as many as 5 million sheep and cattle to the Siberian area of Russia, where Tuva is located. This helped to feed the territory, whose climate is even harsher than Mongolia's. Beginning in the early 1990s, however, Russia began imposing taxes on imports and requiring all transactions to be conducted with actual money, which had not been the case under communism. The Tuvans could no longer afford Mongolian livestock and were going hungry.

As a result, the Tuvans have turned to stealing. The angered Mongolians have responded by counter-stealing. In only one year, Tuvan cattle thieves stole 2,056 head of cattle, while the retaliating Mongolians stole 719. The Tuvans also steal horses. Once the animals are across the border in Tuva, an established ring of slaughterer-criminals quickly prepares the meat for sale. This is to hide all evidence of it being stolen, like Mongolian branding. The meat is then sold for a high price in Siberian markets. Almost every day, an illegal border crossing has occurred from Tuva to Mongolia. The Mongolians illegally crossed into Tuva about half as often. Both the Mongolian and Russian governments have promised to devote more energy to border patrol, but the guards are often concerned about protecting their own lives and, therefore, do not interfere.

The situation has created terror among northern Mongolian herdsmen. "It was already well past midnight when a dog barked," said D. Munkhbaatar, a 27-year-old Mongolian herder. "I came out and saw in distance [sic] several horse riders. When they came closer, they suddenly shot at me several times. Then they broke into our *ger* and began firing." His cousins quickly blew out the candles to obscure the shooters' view and protected Munkhbaatar's brothers by lying flat over them. Munkhbaatar's mother and father were shot dead in their beds. The thieves stole 68 cows and two horses.

The Tuvans have also taken hostages, including children. Herder G. Damjin was kidnapped, taken to Tuva, beaten and interrogated for two days about what had happened to cattle stolen by Mongolians. He was then shot in both legs and left on the Mongolian border. By the time he was discovered lying in the snow, his arms and legs were severely frostbitten.

The local herdsmen have tried petitioning the government (one had 88 horses stolen while he went to Ulaanbaatar to do this), but as many as one-third of the families have now given up and moved away.

DŽUD

In recent years Mongolia has been plagued by natural disasters known as *dzud*. There are at least three types of *dzud*: black, white, and iron. Black *dzud*, or "black death," is a phenomenon of the warmer months and occurs when drought limits the growth of grass for grazing. White *dzud*, "white death," occurs when unusually heavy winter snow prevents animals from grazing on the grass below it. In normal winters without *dzud*, the snow does not fall heavily enough on the steppe to prevent grazing. Iron *dzud* occurs when thawing and re-freezing form a layer of ice (not just snow) over the ground. It also reduces physical access to grass.

In 1998, more than a third of Mongolia's grain crop got buried under snow, preventing access. In the winter of 1999–2000, 2.7 million head of livestock died because of *dzud*. More than 2,400 families lost all of their livestock. In the winter of 2000–01, another 2 million livestock died. In addition to starvation, many animals, frozen into the snow, died of cold. Even those animals that survive such a period of dense snowcover often miscarry because their bodies cannot nourish the fetus, or are too weak to even make it on their own to spring.

The recent disaster was perhaps the severest in Mongolians' memory. "I have seen many things in my life but have never heard from elders of anything like this when white and black *dzud* come together," said one herder. Only 10 percent or so of Mongolians have insurance for their herds, so most of the losses are not compensated. The animal losses not only deprive herders of their wealth but also make it difficult to preserve what wealth remains. Without horses, it is difficult for Mongolians to herd the animals that have survived. Without yaks or camels, it is hard to carry *ger* and other belongings to better pastures. Without any animals at all, herders do not have the dairy products so important to their diet. *Dzud* affects Mongolians in ways other than killing livestock. It cuts off communication among herding camps, as there are almost no telephone lines, plowed roads, or mobile phones on the steppe. *Dzud* makes finding wood or dung for fuel to battle the harsh cold practically impossible. Families are then driven to burn wooden tables, beds, and even the structure of the *ger* itself to provide warmth.

The recent *dzud* was severe in itself, but the economic conditions caused by the transition from communism also made herders especially vulnerable. For one, many of the people herding now are novices. The Soviets had encouraged Mongolian industry. When they left, the machinery to make manufactured goods and the consumers to buy them left too, and many industrial workers were among the jobless. In response, the number of herders in Mongolia tripled between 1990 and 2000. Ochir, an ex-timber worker who became a herder, summed it up: "In this situation, what do you do? Our national heritage is herding. . . . We live in tents in the countryside and raise animals . . . So I bought a few sheep and goats." Not only are small herds always vulnerable, but Ochir had no idea what to do when things went wrong. He was not accustomed to planning for tough times and emergencies. The Communist government had always done that, storing fodder for the winter, having the equipment to transport it to the countryside, and providing veterinary services. Ochir admits he was at a loss. "When bad weather hit I was caught completely by surprise. I didn't have a winter shelter. I didn't have enough hay or

Twenty-five-year-old Aryuntor herds sheep near his family's ger *on the Hurandel Hills in Mongolia in November 1998. Aryuntor has decided to return to the nomadic life, after struggling to make ends meet in the nearby city of Zuunmod.* (AP/Wide World Photos/Greg Baker)

fodder. I didn't have enough horses or any camels to move on to a better place. So what happened? Everything died."

Increased herd sizes as well as increased numbers of inexperienced herders have contributed to the *dzud* disaster. Under communism, the government controlled herd size. Since communism fell, herd sizes have increased as herders compete with each other. The Communist government also provided a market for animal products in other Communist countries, and ran factories for processing animals into useful goods. In recent years the market for livestock has suffered, so animals have remained alive, needing grass, that otherwise would have been slaughtered. Experts estimate that Mongolia's land can support 63 million sheep or their equivalent in other animals. As of 1998, there was the equivalent of 69.2 million sheep living in Mongolia. Competition for good grazing land has become very stiff. Normally, nomads depend on each other and cooperate in the event of a disaster. This time, herders in one county actually took up arms to prevent *dzud*-stricken neighbors from sharing their pastures.

Forecasters predict only more of the same. The winter of 2002–03 was expected to bring another *dzud* with it; the government was recommending that herders slaughter their underweight livestock in advance rather than watch them die with no meat on them. The government has also been providing what disaster relief it can, including some nutritional assistance to children whose families have had little food. Nonprofits are encouraging herders to form larger (larger than a *khot ail*) communities to replace the ones that departed with the Communist era. "The one thing you can say about the Communists is that they knew what they were doing," said David Dyer of the Gobi Regional Growth Initiative. "That paternalistic attitude may have taken all self-motivation out of the people here. . . . They must realize that they must get together so that specializations can develop: people to grow hay, some to market the products, and that way to spread the cost of the vet[erinarian] between several families."

Underlying environmental problems also need to be addressed. The Ministry of Nature and the Environment believes that the livestock economy will be threatened in the long-term as much by land degradation as by *dzud*. It estimated in 2001 that 78 percent of Mongolia's land was in a state of decline due to overgrazing. "Decline" means soil degradation, vegetation degradation, and eventual desertification. In the 10 years between 1991 and 2001, the ministry believed, the percentage of desert-like land in Mongolia increased by 3.4 percent—a significant amount of good grazing land to lose when livestock are already underfed. Groups are considering ways of managing what pastureland remains better, as well as managing herd sizes.

NOTES

p. 83 "'meat is for men . . .'" Donald R. DeGlopper, "The Society and Its Environment," in *Mongolia: A Country Study* (Washington, D.C.: Library of Congress Research Division, 1991), p. 76.

p. 84 "There are approximately . . ." Mayhew, *Mongolia*, p. 30.

p. 86 "To satisfy weight-based . . ." "Mongolia: Camels." Available on-line. URL: http://www.halcyon.com/mongolia/camels.html. Site updated January 29, 1995.

p. 88 "Mongolia provides about 20 percent . . ." Gobi Cashmere. "Company Overview." Available on-line. URL: http://www.spc.gov.mn/compnies/gobi/gobi_marketing.htm. Site updated September 18, 2002.

p. 89 "Cuts of meat . . ." consulate of Mongolia. "Traditions and Customs." Available on-line. URL: http://www.mongolia.org.hk/country_info-6-01.htm. Site updated January 30, 2002.

p. 92 "'It was already well . . .'" Quoted in "Unquiet Northern Border," in *Mongolia Today*, Issue 3. Available on-line. URL:http://www.mongoliatoday.com/issue/3/northern_borders.html. Posted 1999–2002.

p. 92 "In 1998, more than a third . . ." "Winter in Mongolia," in *Mongolia Today*, Issue 2. Available on-line. URL: http://www.mongoliatoday.com/issue/2/winter.html. Posted 1999–2002.

pp. 92–93 "In the winter of 2000–2001 . . ." David Hadrill, "The International Response to Emergencies in Mongolia," on Tropical Agriculture Association's Talk page, November 30, 2001. Available on-line. URL: http://www.taa.org.uk/TAAScotland/MongoliaHadrill.htm.

p. 93 "'I have seen . . .'" Quoted in "Disaster Aftermath,'" in *Mongolia Today*, Issue 3. Available on-line. URL:http://www.mongoliatoday.com/issue/3/dzud_disaster.html. Posted 1999–2002.

p. 93 "Only 10 percent or so . . ." *Mongolia Today*, Issue 3.

pp. 93–94 "'In this situation . . .'" Chris Anderson, "Taking Steppes to Survive," on Scotsman. com, August 4, 2002. Available on-line. URL: http://news.scotsman.com/features.cfm?id=836472002.

p. 94 "Experts estimate that Mongolia's land . . ." "National Seminar Discusses Sustainable Grassland Management for Mongolia," on United Nations in Mongolia news site, October, 2001. Available on-line. URL: http://www.un-mongolia.mn/news/.

p. 94 "This time, herders . . ." "White Death Strikes Again," in *Mongolia Today*, Issue 5. Available on-line. URL:http://www.mongoliatoday.com/issue/5/dzud.html. Posted 1999–2002.

p. 95 "The winter of 2002–03 . . ." "Zud Disaster Inevitable," in *Mongol Messenger*, September 3, 2002.

p. 95 "'The one thing you can say . . .'" Chris Anderson, "Taking Steppes to Survive," on Scotsman.com, August 4, 2002. Available on-line. URL:http://news.scotsman.com/features.cfm?id=836472002.

p. 95 "It estimated in 2001 . . ." "National Seminar Discusses Sustainable Grassland Management for Mongolia," on United Nations in Mongolia news page, October, 2001. Available on-line. URL: http://www.un-mongolia.mn/news/.

p. 95 "In the 10 years . . ." "National Seminar Discusses Sustainable Grassland Management for Mongolia," October, 2001.

7

CULTURE IN TRANSITION

Mongolian culture today is a strange mix of the traditional and the modern, the old and the new—although, in Mongolia's case, the old is sometimes the new. The Communists suppressed many old Mongolian traditions, forcing the country into the bland mold of the Communist bloc, with its gray buildings, standardized apartments, factories, and lack of individuality. Since the fall of communism, old cultural habits and celebrations, once suppressed or frowned upon, have revived. Religion in all its ceremonial richness has returned. So have traditional marriage rites, holidays, and customs. Some traditions were not suppressed by the Communists, and they have survived in modern Mongolia. Opening Mongolia to the larger world has also ushered in modernity, reforming certain aspects of society, such as communications, music (see also chapter 8), and education. At the same time it has created new problems for Mongolians, problems mostly absent from the former Communist world. Capitalism produces higher highs and lower lows, and those Mongolians adversely affected by it are now also suffering from alcoholism, domestic violence, and homelessness, among other problems.

Religion

Before the era of the khans (Genghis and his descendants) most Mongolians practiced shamanism, a form of traditional nature worship. By the time of Kublai Khan's reign (1260–1294), representatives of Buddhism,

Christianity, and Islam had begun to influence the khans' court and Mongolian society. But it was not until 1578 and Altan Khan's official conversion that Buddhism took hold in Mongolia.

Since the transition to democracy, Buddhism and Mongolia's minority religions have flourished. The Dalai Lama, leader of the sect of Buddhism that Mongolia subscribes to, has visited, attracting crowds of hundreds of thousands. More than a hundred monasteries have reopened. Without trained lamas, or spiritual leaders, of its own, Mongolia is welcoming teachers from India, Tibet, and elsewhere.

Buddhism is a religion of balance and self-control, perhaps more inward-looking than any of the other major world religions. There are almost countless ways of expressing the goals of Buddhism, but one is

> Abandon negative action;
> Create perfect virtue;
> Subdue your own mind.

The Buddha teaches that life on earth is filled with suffering, caused by over-attachment to earthly things and people that are bound to pass away from us. We can escape this suffering by following the teachings of Buddha. This is summed up in the first two of the Four Noble Truths of

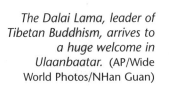

The Dalai Lama, leader of Tibetan Buddhism, arrives to a huge welcome in Ulaanbaatar. (AP/Wide World Photos/NHan Guan)

TIBETAN BUDDHISM

In the last several centuries B.C. and in the first centuries A.D., Buddhism spread widely throughout Asia. Communications across vast spaces and altitudes were not well-developed at this time, and the human cultures Buddhism reached and influenced differed from one another, so Buddhism developed in different ways in different places. Tibet, where the intersection of India and Asia quietly pushes the Himalayas higher by the day, provided an ideally isolated environment for Buddhism to flourish.

Buddhism touched Tibet a few times in the early centuries A.D. and established itself there by the late 700s A.D. Tibetan Buddhism is distinguished by its relatively stronger emphasis on love and compassion as opposed to more technical thinking about morality. It also employs yoga more intensively than some Buddhist traditions do. In yoga as practiced in Tibet, for example, the body is seen as able to exist in three different ways. In one sense the body exists as part of the physical, external world, made of the same material as the rest of it. In another the body feels partly connected to the external world and partly sufficient in itself, taking things in through the senses and enjoying them internally. In the third sense, one exists deep within one's body, having experienced things outside it and resolved them into subtle and deep truths capable of outliving the body's fragile physical form.

Tibetan Buddhism, tragically, is now a religious tradition in exile from its homeland. China currently occupies Tibet militarily, represses all religion, and has driven spiritual leaders such as the Dalai Lama out.

Buddhism: the truth of suffering and the cause of suffering. The last two of the Four Noble Truths are the end of suffering and its causes and the path to that ending. The end of suffering and its causes is known as Nirvana, a word which has entered the English language. The path to Nirvana is the true work of Buddhists, and, once again, can be described in a variety of ways.

Simply, it is known as the Middle Way between extremes of self-indulgence and self-denial. Buddhists do not believe, as some groups of Hindus and members of other religions do, in asceticism—gaining a higher state of spiritual awareness through denying oneself food, shelter, clothing, and so forth. They also do not believe in complete abandonment to earthly pleasures. The path to Nirvana can also be described as involving the Three Higher Trainings: ethical discipline, meditative stabilization, and wisdom. Each of these, in turn, involves elements of the Eightfold Path. Ethical discipline includes (1) right speech, (2) right activity (actions that are not harmful to others), and (3) right livelihood (obtaining one's food/money through honest and nonharmful means). Meditative stabilization involves (4) right effort, (5) right mindfulness (getting rid of laziness and over-excitement), and (6) right *samadhi* (concentration upon virtuous things). Wisdom includes (7) right view and (8) right thought (the ability to explain the path to others and hope that they too will be free from suffering). Considering this path, one can understand why Buddhism acted as a pacifying influence on the formerly warlike Mongolians.

But the Buddhist world does not consist solely of oneself and one's own thoughts. Unlike the major Western religions of Judaism, Islam, and Christianity, it does not have one God but rather many gods and godlike creatures. These include buddhas, gods (*devas*), demigods (*asuras*), spirits (*pretas*), and demons (*narakas*), among others. Among the buddhas, there are some very well known ones. Buddhism's loose counterpart to Jesus Christ and Muhammad, for example, is the "historical Buddha," Siddartha Gautama. Gautama was a prince who lived in the fifth century B.C. in what is now southern Nepal. Distraught by human suffering, he gave up his wealth and gained enlightenment through meditation. Other buddhas include the "future" buddha (expected to return to earth in a few thousand years), contemplation buddhas, the buddha of longevity, the Medicine Buddha, and the compassionate buddha. The Dalai Lama is considered an incarnation of the compassionate buddha. The religion also teaches that buddhahood can be attained by people practicing the steps described above.

Unlike Islam, Buddhism does not shun images of its deities but, rather, embraces them. As discussed in chapter 8, page 127, Buddhist texts prescribe specific proportions for statues and images of deities. Partly because the Buddha may take so many forms, Buddhist art is extraordinarily varied and complex. For example, the historical Buddha is usually pictured sitting cross-legged on a throne made of lotus flowers. His right hand touches the ground, while his left hand holds a bowl for begging. Representations of the buddha of compassion attempt to show the deity's empathy in a physical way, through the color white or through showing the buddha with a thousand arms, each with an all-understanding eye on its palm. The buddha of wisdom, Manjushri, is depicted in gold, which is intended to illuminate the mind as the golden Sun illuminates the Earth. Manjushri also holds a flaming sword, to cut through ignorance. Tara, the Savior, has 21 different manifestations, symbolizes purity and fertility, and is thought to grant wishes. Green Tara is associated with night, while white Tara is associated with day. Mahakala is the god of wealth, and is believed by Mongolians to be the guardian of the nomad's tent.

In the wake of communism's fall, other religions have also thrived. Among these, which include Islam and the Nestorian, Mormon, and Catholic forms of Christianity, the most important is Shamanism. Shamanism is a descendant of the traditional worship practiced by Mongolians before the time of the khans. Shamanism has as its goal a life in balance with the natural world. This leads believers to be very aware of their orientation—in the sense of the compass directions, but also with respect to the sky, the world, the world below ground, and one's physical position within the home. Shamanists see divine force in all of nature. Father Heaven (Tenger Etseg), they believe, is in the blue sky that is visible most of the time in Mongolia, in the almost ever-present wind, in lightning, and in meteorites. Shamanists see Mother Earth (Gazar Eej) in trees, minerals, and plants.

Religious leaders of Shamanism are known as shamans, if male, or shamankas, if female. Becoming a shaman or shamanaka is not believed to be a matter of choice. Rather, the spirits choose the person. Future shamans are identified by unusual behavior, such as trances or visions. The chosen must then learn to communicate with the spirits by further removing themselves from society—through fasting, for example, or living as hermits for periods of time. Once someone becomes a shaman or shamanaka, he or she helps to cure diseases, banish evil spirits, find lost animals, and provide guidance concerning daily activities.

One material aspect of folk worship is the *ovoo*, a small shrine found in the countryside. It is a pyramid-shaped pile of rocks to which passersby add offerings. These may include vodka bottles, silk scarves (usually blue, the color of the sacred sky), money, sweets, or tobacco. Sometimes a moose or yak head is placed on top of the pyramid. When coming upon an *ovoo*, one should walk around it three times clockwise and then make an offering. Digging, hunting, and logging nearby are prohibited. Mongolians believe that those who disrespect *ovoo* may become ill and even die.

Ovoo also are occasionally the site of more formal worship ceremonies led by shamans. These involve prayers, pouring *airag*, or liquor, on the *ovoo*, and making other offerings to it. A small feast or celebration follows, perhaps with horse racing or wrestling. Such rituals are generally held to celebrate spring or encourage rain, the growth of plentiful grass, and good hunting.

While religion is flourishing in Mongolia, some stumbling blocks to its practice remain. The constitution and specific laws are protective of religious freedom but still require religions to register with the government. This process subjects religions to time-wasting bureaucracy at the least and harassment and demands for bribes at the worst. There are several steps in the registration process, which can result in many different officials requesting bribes. And registration at the national level does not even guarantee freedom from bureaucratic interference. Groups wishing to practice in the countryside may be required to register locally as well. National officials have also threatened groups with withdrawing their registration if they do not continue to pay bribes. As of 2002, only two-thirds of the 260 temples, churches, and mosques—including 90 Buddhist, 40 Christian, four Baha'i, and one Islamic—founded since 1990 had succeeded in gaining registration.

Sports, Games, and Holidays

Athletic competitions and other activities are closely associated with holidays in Mongolia, where the nomadic lifestyle did not permit large groups of people to take time off to participate in sports except on special occasions. While these were not suppressed by the Communists nearly to the extent of religion, some established events were renamed, many modern sports were banned, and it was not easy for Mongolians to compete internationally. This did have some positive effects, preserving traditional moves in wrestling, for example, which were forgotten elsewhere. Now Mongolians are free to play or celebrate as they want—either in traditional ways, modern ones, or in a combination of the two.

Sports are very popular in Mongolia. The three traditional or "manly" sports are horse racing, wrestling, and archery. Despite the category under which it is included, wrestling is the only one of three sports that women do not participate in. The three manly sports are the backbone of Mongolia's great summer festival, Naadam. Naadam lasts through July and August, with sporting events taking place throughout the country. The most important Naadam festival is held in Ulaanbaatar. The history of Naadam itself goes back almost 400 years, although it was suspended during the Communist era. But great celebrations with games, known by other names, were being held in Mongolia at the same time as gladiators were fighting in Rome.

In the last few years B.C., a tribe called the Hunnu, known to the western world as the Huns, celebrated games before beginning and after winning wars. When new kings were crowned, people made sacrifices to the sky god, or received foreign visitors, games were part of the festivities. The games were well established by the time of Genghis Khan (around 1200), and fit in well with his military agenda. Riding, wrestling, and archery skills were applicable in war. According to storytellers, one tribal ruler wanted to test Genghis's military abilities before swearing allegiance to him, so he challenged Genghis to shoot a flag from 4,500 feet, or almost one mile, away. Genghis shot it in one attempt, and received the ruler's allegiance.

Horse riding, the first of the manly sports, is one of a herder's job requirements, a crucial means of transportation on the steppe, and a source of entertainment, so children learn to ride almost as soon as they can walk. In fact, the riders in horse races are typically children between five and 13 years old. The categories of races are based not on the age of the rider but on the age of the horse, with older horses racing for longer distances of almost 20 miles. The races are conducted not on tracks but in the open countryside.

Mongolian racehorses are not the skittish, coddled thoroughbreds that run in the Kentucky Derby or other European and American races. On the contrary, Mongolian racehorses work with their herder-riders when not racing. But prior to important races like those at Naadam, the horses are given special treatment—the best pasture, little hard racing, and swim training (easy on the joints, good for the muscles).

Some 18,000 horses compete in Naadam races. The race begins with the audience singing traditional songs and a song, or *gingo*, sung by the rider him- or herself. After the race, riders or members of the audience scrape sweat off the horses' backs with a pelican beak, and the winners are feted with poems and *airag*.

The last rider to finish the race also is singled out. The losing horse's slowness is attributed to its failure to lose enough fat during training, so the horse is jokingly given the title "rich stomach" and a dried sheep stomach is attached to it. The audience then sings a song that blames the loss of the race on everything but the horse, such as unfortunately placed sand dunes, and offers hope for the following year.

> Because of a foolish owner, the reins were too short . . .
> The rider was too young, and the whip too short.
> Too many sand dunes happened on the way,
> As well as many hills and ravines
> As always there were obstacles.
> And though the jockey tried hard,
> To overcome all of them, still too many remained.
> The young colt lagged behind all
> But next year, the rider will be ahead of 10,000 horses.

Wrestling is an even bigger Naadam event than horse racing, with 30,000 people competing. Mongolian wrestling differs from modern Olympic wrestling in that it has no weight categories, no time limit (until recently matches could last some three hours), and the outfits worn by the wrestlers are highly unusual. Wrestlers are supposed to imitate the mythical *garuda* bird in their stances. Victory comes when any part of the opposing wrestler's body other than the soles of his shoes or the palms of his hands touches the ground. The wrestlers wear short embroidered "pants" resembling a Speedo bathing suit and a jacket that bares the chest. Both are brightly colored. Supposedly, the jacket is styled to detect a possible female competitor because a woman disguised as a man once trounced all the male wrestlers. The wrestlers also wear slouchy, leather pointed-toe boots and sometimes a pointy hat prior to beginning the match. After the match, the loser must walk under the right arm of the winner during a victory lap. The winner then performs the eagle dance. Wrestlers who win multiple rounds are given titles such as "falcon," "elephant," "lion," and, in one case, "Eye-pleasing nationally famous mighty and invincible giant."

The training provided to Mongolian wrestlers has enabled them to compete at the international level in sumo wrestling, even introducing innovations to the sport. One Mongolian wrestler, D. Batbayar, competes extensively in Japan, where he is described as a "supermarket of tricks." Some of these include moves that were preserved in Mongolian wrestling but forgotten by the Japanese, enabling Batbayar to take his opponents unawares. Batbayar has become an Asian celebrity, sharing Mongolian songs with audiences in Japan and publishing a book of memoirs.

Archery is the Naadam event with the fewest participants, usually about 2,000. Traditional archery games came in two forms. In one, marksmen hung leather balls from a stick, challenging competitors to shoot the balls from farther and farther away. Another form involved shooting at hanging sheepskins while astride a speeding horse. In today's competitions, marksmen attempt to shoot into colored leather rings arranged on

Mongolian wrestling is not for the self-conscious. Three wrestlers of Ulaanbaatar, 1950s. (Courtesy Library of Congress)

the ground. Women stand closer to the targets than men do. The bow is made of horn, bark, and wood. The arrow is usually made from willow, and feathers are from local birds of prey, especially vultures.

Other traditional games include *shagai*, in which sheep anklebones are used as dice; a hockey-like game in which players on a field of ice kick a puck-like object made of camel or ox anklebone; shooting bones, again using anklebones; and horse catching (what it sounds like). In a twist on the familiar form of chess, the Mongolian version may use a khan for the king piece, a lion or tiger for the queen, horse-drawn carts for the castle, a fierce bull-camel or mother camel and young for the bishop, and a boy for the pawn. Craftsmen carve the pieces for fine sets from sandalwood or ivory.

In addition, Mongolians enjoy familiar modern sports such as football, basketball, volleyball, soccer, gymnastics, skiing, skateboarding, biking, hang gliding, and mountain climbing. In Ulaanbaatar, for example, children have learned skateboarding moves from watching cable television. They congregate on the steps of the parliament building to practice, share tricks, and meet friends. Similarly, from watching TV Mongolians have

Archery, one of the three "manly" sports, is excelled at by women. (Courtesy of the United Nations)

adopted American basketball stars as their own heroes. One reporter told a Mongolian teenager, Zorigbaataar, that his name was Michael. "Ah yes, Michael Jordan! Chee-cah-go BULLS!" Zorigbaataar cried. "I am Mongolian Michael Jordan," he continued, displaying Bulls garb. Mongolia now has its own professional basketball league.

The major Mongolian holiday other than Naadam, Tsagaan Sar (White Month, or New Year's), is at the opposite end of the calendar and emphasizes togetherness rather than competition. It falls according to the lunar calendar sometime between late January and early March. The Communists renamed it "The Day of Cooperative Members" in 1960 to commemorate the socialist change in the economy, but it was revived under its traditional name in 1989. In fact, the holiday has been celebrated in Mongolia since the time of Kublai Khan or longer. Marco Polo remarked on it in his writings about Kublai's court:

> On that day all vassal countries and people presented the Khan with gold and silver, pearls and precious stones, as well as expensive white fabrics. Particularly impressive were the white steeds, elephants and camels which the Emperor received on that day. All the people, the nobility and ordinary folk alike, also exchanged gifts, and merry-making took place all through the day, so that the following year should be joyous and prosperous.

Preparations begin a month in advance. Tsagaan Sar involves feasting, so families stockpile dairy products and other provisions. Men make repairs to animal sheds. They and the *ger* are cleaned. Women make new *del* (robes) for their families, as people are supposed to welcome the new year wearing new clothes.

Bituun, meaning "to close down," is the New Year's Eve feast. By the time it occurs, all business of the past year should have been resolved. Debts should have been paid, and strained relationships mended. Family sit at the dinner table according to age and hierarchy. Before beginning the meal, the host slices a leg of lamb and gives everyone a piece. Then he breaks the bone and exposes the marrow, symbolizing the end of one year and the beginning of another. The group also feast on oblong pastries piled up in pyramids and decorated with sweets and dried curd, on meat-filled dumplings, milk rice pap with raisins, *airag*, and more. The dinner usually goes on for a long time, and even dogs receive extra bones.

Feasting, ritual greetings, and games continue the next day. The whole first month following the New Year, in fact, is a holiday. Herders deliberately graze their animals far from camp before the New Year so that the grass near the camp will be available for the month after New Year's. This way, the men can spend more time at camp celebrating and less time traveling to faraway fields every day. Children living away from home are expected to visit their parents during the month, no matter how far they must travel to do so. There are also important taboos—things not to be done during the New Year celebration:

> Don't call a man by his nickname, argue, hunt or kill cattle.
> Don't eat before the host allows it.
> Don't get drunk.
> Don't wear a knife or weapon.
> Don't stay the night.

Besides Naadam and Tsagaan Sar, other Mongolian holidays include those related to the nation and political life. Genghis Khan's birth, for example, has become a national holiday. In 2002, Mongolians celebrated the 840th anniversary (government officials who tried to celebrate the 800th in 1962 had their posts eliminated) of Genghis's birth with art exhibits, wrestling competitions, and by launching construction of a monument to the great Khan in Ulaanbaatar. President Bagabandi proclaimed Genghis "the star of the Mongolian nation and man of the millennium." The memorial, in the Park of Culture and Leisure, will consist of seven stone tents on a rock pedestal almost 300 feet wide and almost 200 feet tall. A 60-foot-high statue of Genghis surrounded by statues of his nine closest military advisers will be the centerpiece of the monument.

Holidays also include those related to traditional customs (housewarming, *airag* day, etc.), those related to animals (day of horseherds, day of sheep-shearing and branding of animals, etc.), and family events (naming a baby, first haircut, birthdays, weddings, funerals). Babies, for example, are named at a ceremony occurring three days after birth. The baby is bathed by the mother or grandmother in meat broth. A monk then prays over the baby and dunks the child in holy water. Relatives bring food and gifts. At the first haircut, three years later, relatives gather again. The child's oldest relative takes the first cut, offers the child good wishes, and gives him or her a gift. Others follow. The child's mother gathers the locks of cut hair in a silk scarf and sews them inside the child's pillow.

Marriage is probably the most elaborate of these family rituals, and is celebrated in a variety of ways according to location (various regions of the country have different traditions; urban celebrations may be different from rural ones), family, religiosity, wealth, and the couple's inclination. Mongolian weddings today represent a rejection of the Communist way of doing things, replaced by a combination of traditional and modern customs.

For one, many Mongolians are being choosier about potential mates than they were in Communist times. Then, jobs, income, and health care were guaranteed no matter whom one married, so qualities like intelligence, ambition, and work ethic were less important. "It was different at the time of our parents. Life was guaranteed and we believed that there was no bad men," says Bobia, a university student. Most of her friends were now looking for responsibility and potential for success in a spouse.

In Communist times, weddings for city people were likely to have been conducted in a European ceremony in the government-built Palace of Marriage Ceremony. Now, the palace has been refurbished with more Mongolian decoration, including paintings and statues of Buddha that before would have been illegal. The palace also contains the small traditional Mongolian fires, *tulga*. These symbolize the joining of the bride's and groom's flames into a single eternal fire. Before getting married, a couple often consults a lama to ask for a blessing. If the lama foresees tough times for the couple, he may perform additional rites. These days, couples prefer to get married on Buddhist holy days. The most popular of these are Dashnyam and Baljinnyam, celebrated on a single day in the fall. In 1999, 98 couples were married on this day in a single chapel. The first wedding had to take place at 4 A.M. and the last at 11 P.M. in order to fit them all in.

Some city couples are actually going the opposite direction and opting to stay together but not get married, or at least not have a wedding. "I asked my girlfriend to marry me. If she wants, she just can take her suitcase with her and move to my place," says Tumen, a medical student. The increasing divorce rate may have motivated this trend. "I know many divorced, after having nice weddings," says Tumen. Divorced people who find someone new may also feel too old for a wedding, since weddings in Mongolia are viewed as primarily for the young. The extremely low number of divorces prior to the 1990s may have created this assumption, which perhaps will now begin to change. The average age for getting married has already risen from 18 to 20 to 21 to 24, according to an employee of the Wedding Palace.

In the countryside, the couple's parents may be more involved, and the ceremony held in a *ger*. When parents feel that their son is an adult, they may build him a *ger*. If the son finds a woman to marry, his relatives will go to her parents and ask for her hand. Sometimes her parents will refuse, and the groom's relatives will have to ask again and again for several days. If and when the bride's parents finally agree, the groom's relatives will give them presents. The two sides will agree on a day for the bride to be escorted to the groom's new *ger*. Before she leaves home, the bride receives milk from her mother. The bride offers prayers in her new home, and then the wedding celebration begins. It often lasts for many days.

The countryside is also the stronghold of traditional Mongolian customs, manners, gestures, and ways of interacting, although some carry over into urban life as well. Of these customs, hospitality to visitors, including strangers, is perhaps the most important. "Happy is he who often has guests; cheerful is the home near which stand the horses of visitors," goes a Mongolian proverb. On the steppe, shelter and food are the difference between life and death, even in summer. Therefore, the door of a *ger* is always open, and guests are welcome to enter and have a snack or a nap even if none of the *ger*'s inhabitants is home. Knocking is never required, and it is not considered rude to arrive even in the middle of the night. Older or esteemed guests are met and seen off, if possible, at the door of the *ger* or fence, if there happens to be one. Hosts do not come outside to welcome younger guests.

If the owners are home, it is customary for them to offer guests some hot tea and perhaps a plate of cheese, fresh cream, and candies (even if the guests arrive in the middle of the night). Guests should accept these offerings before beginning conversation. Then, the guest should inquire about the health of the host, the health of the family's animals, and the quality of the grazing. Mongolians always answer optimistically, even if this is not realistic. The host customarily inquires where the visitor is from and where he or she is heading. If the guest is not in a hurry, the host will invite him or her to spend the night. While guests, even Westerners, are not expected to compensate the host for their stay, small gifts are appropriate. Large gifts can be perceived as insulting, implying either that the host is poor or that he would not be hospitable without being compensated for it. Therefore, it is best to give candy, or a little candy money, to the children of the house, or milk or other dairy products to the elderly.

Mongolians also have rituals for interacting with people they already know and expect to see. When Mongolian men greet each other, especially to transact business, it is customary for them to exchange snuff bottles and take pinches at the beginning and end of the meeting. When receiving the snuff, or other gift or food, one should use both hands. Often, the recipient extends his or her right hand, using the left hand to support the right elbow.

Mongolians in cities use a Western-style handshake. A traditional greeting is more likely to be used in the countryside if the two people greeting one another differ in age or status. In this case, the younger or lower-status person gently supports the forearms of the other person. Social kissing is similarly governed by rank and age. Older people may kiss younger people on the cheeks in greeting and parting, but not vice versa. Friends may kiss in greeting, but not in public. Hugging is considered intimate and reserved for lovers. In parting, hosts bow and press their hands together palm-to-palm at chest height, wave, or give a handshake once again.

Many gestures are, by contrast, forbidden. Pointing with one finger, for example, is impolite. To point something out or beckon someone to come, all the fingers are extended and the palm faces down. Crossing one's legs is taboo, as is staring into the eyes of an elder. A Westerner was once hospitalized for injuries received after he moved a Mongolian's hat in a bar—this is also taboo.

Mongolians are known for their unwillingness to show emotion. Open expression of feelings and snap judgments are highly disfavored. Patience, thoughtfulness, and tolerance are highly valued, on the other hand. "Shifting emotions and tempers are sinful, while understanding is a good deed," remarked one older Mongolian. Some of the young, since the transition to democracy, hope to change this. "I think American kids are very free and mature, they can talk openly and on the same level with their parents. Mongolian kids are too shy," said Oggy, a teenager. Nonetheless, even Mongolia's hard rockers remain worshipful toward their parents (see chapter 8, page 132).

Gift-giving is an important Mongolian tradition, more symbolic than lavish. Food and hospitality to *ger* visitors are, obviously, gifts, for which nothing is expected in return. Mongolians also exchange physical tokens of good feeling. On New Year's Day, for example, guests leaving the *ger* after a visit receive a small gift. The oldest son also presents his mother with a blue silk scarf, symbolizing respect and good wishes. Scarves of other colors are also common gifts. White symbolizes purity of thought, and yellow symbolizes longevity and prosperity.

Another new, very important development affects Mongolians' connection to their pasts and to family: the revival of family names (known to Westerners as "last" names or surnames). In 1991, President Ochirbat issued a decree to revive family names. People were free to either begin using their old family name or to adopt a new one.

Because family names had been forbidden for 65 years, many people did not know what theirs used to be. One way to do research was to go to the place where one's parents were born and probe the memories of elderly locals. If this did not work, Mongolians could consult a guide that was published to help with name research. It listed 1,260 family names and provided maps of where certain family names were common.

Many people either gave up on such research or preferred to take a new name. Many people took the Genghis Khan family name, Borjigid (Wolfmaster), without any evidence of relation to him. Others took the names of popular animals, such as Eagle and Crow. Some took names of professions like Smith, Hunter, or Camelbreeder.

The unusual Mongolian calendar also endures. It is similar to the Chinese calendar. There are 12 years, named for twelve animals, in the cycle. Some are considered hard or male, and some are considered easy or female. Male and female alternate; the cycle begins with the masculine year of the mouse, followed by the years of the ox, tiger, rabbit, dragon, snake, horse, sheep, monkey, cock, dog, and pig. Thus, mouse, dragon, horse, monkey, tiger, and dog are considered masculine years, while ox, rabbit, snake, sheep, cock, and pig are feminine years. By the same token, the hours of the day are also divided into 12 periods of two hours each, corresponding to these same animals. Thus, the "hour" of the mouse is from midnight to 2 A.M., the ox from 2 to 4 A.M., the tiger from 4 to 6 A.M., and so on.

Modern Culture

One of the hallmarks of free societies is a proliferation of media—newspapers, magazines, radio stations, and TV stations, each with its own perspective and consumers. Mongolia has experienced tremendous growth in this area since the end of communism. In Communist days, *Unen* (Truth; the Soviet counterpart, *Pravda,* meant the same thing), the journal of the Communist Party, was one of few available. Now, the daily newspapers include *Ardiin Erkh* (People's Right); *Zunny Medee* (Century News); *Odriin Sonin* (Daily News); *and Onoodor* (Today). In addition, Mongolia has English newspapers and magazines: *The Mongol Messenger* (www. mongolnet.mn/mglmsg/index.html), *The UB Post* (www.ulaanbaatar.net/ ubpost), and *Ger Magazine* (www.un-mongolia.mn/ger-mag). As of 2000, there were more than 800 registered newspapers, a huge number for a population of approximately 2.5 million.

There is slightly less variety in the audio and video categories. Televisions are widely owned (though not multiple sets per household). Satellite and cable TV are available to the few who can afford them; others must settle for Ulaanbaatar TV, Mongol TB, and some Russian stations, all mainly playing Russian movies, hours of wrestling, news, and documentaries. Radio remains extremely important, as it was during Communist times. Herders rely on it for all-important weather reports as well as news and entertainment. The state-owned radio station continues to be widely heard, and there is an increasing number of small independent stations as well: Jag and the aptly-named Blue Sky, for example. The Voice of America, the British Broadcasting Company (BBC), and Radio Australia broadcast in English.

The Internet has also come to Mongolia. It officially arrived in 1996, when the country got its first Internet service provider. Rivals have since sprung up. Due to a lack of suitable infrastructure and the small number of people with access to computers who are able to take advantage of the network, Internet access was initially extremely expensive (up to $90 a month for an individual in a country where the average annual income is about $405). Therefore, development agencies funded the creation of Internet centers or cafés, hoping to make Mongolians familiar with the Internet so that (1) they would see its usefulness and eventually be willing to pay for it, and (2) there would eventually be enough customers to

Dozens of newspapers now tell "the truth" as they see it, whereas the Commu-nist Party permitted only its version. (AP/Wide World Photos/Greg Baker)

make access cheaper and more widely available. (Government and non-profits initially funded the growth of the Internet in the United States as well.) The strategy worked. The private sector is now opening up Inter-net cafés as for-profit businesses. As of 1999, there were 2,300 individual Internet accounts in the country. Mongolia is also hoping to use the Internet to keep Mongolians all over the world abreast of musical trends and news. The country's first Internet radio station, INFORADIO-105.5 FM, has begun broadcasting at www.inforadio.mn.

Despite the growth, the media do not operate completely freely in Mongolia. Under communism, of course, they were tightly censored, and it has taken a while to implement the constitution's decree that the press shall be free. Initially, as discussed in chapter 3, the Communist Party controlled newspapers by restricting their ability to get newsprint (paper), among other tactics. In 1999, the government passed a sweeping new law to protect the media. It banned censorship and barred state own-ership and financing of media, which is going further even than in the U.S. (public radio, for example, is funded in part by the U.S. government). The law, again, however, proved more optimistic than realistic. Since there had been no agreement on how the media would be privatized, many remained state-owned. Many people complain that despite all the improvements, government is still not as open as it should be, and its control over the media permits this.

Even if the law had been implemented immediately, the press would still have felt hamstrung by other mechanisms of government control. For example, the press finds itself frequently the target of tax audits and libel suits (suits claiming that an article is false and insulting) by government. In the United States, it is practically impossible for government figures to sue the media for libel and slander, even for cartoons and statements that are extremely insulting and obviously false. In Mongolia, this is not so, and there the burden is on the defendant media organization to prove what it wrote or said is true. In response to this condition, some media outlets censor themselves to avoid trouble, refraining from printing things even if they are fairly or completely sure of their truth.

The other main method of distributing information, education, has also undergone changes and privatization since 1990. The communist education system was at the very least successful in teaching the broadest number of people basic skills, and the democratic government has tried to continue that mission. Education is still free, and it is offered for students aged seven to 17. Boarding schools are still available for children of nomadic herders. At the university level, options are increasing. Since 1990, dozens of private universities have been founded, some specializing in areas from computer science to folk medicine. For those who cannot be on-campus, full-time students, groups have funded distance learning. The BBC (British Broadcasting Company) has sponsored TV programs to teach Mongolians English. UNESCO (United Nations Education, Science and Cultural Organization) has sponsored a radio education program to teach herders everything from camel care to marketing skills.

Unfortunately, as with so many other government programs, there are problems. Because of pressures on their families to earn more money, many children are having to drop out of school. The percentage of students completing the 11 years of primary education dropped from 87 percent to 57 percent in the five years between 1990 and 1995 alone. At the university level, males are seeking education at far lower rates than females. In 1999, more than 70 percent of university students were female. Salaries for teachers have also been reportedly so low that they, like other government officials, are vulnerable to corruption. Students can reportedly buy good grades at some schools and universities.

Challenges in Mongolian Society

All the good notwithstanding, the giant changes in Mongolian society of the past 13 years have also brought problems. Economic disruptions in particular have caused problems. Until 1990, Mongolians were taken care of by the state. They were provided with jobs, health care, vacations, *gers* and apartments, and the promise of retirement money in exchange for their liberty. They were not encouraged to think about whether the things they were producing in their jobs were worth buying by anyone, whether the way they were doing their jobs was smart, why they had the job they did, or how they could develop or use their personal skills and talents to compete against others in business. Many, therefore, did not think about these things. Mongolians were encouraged to have large numbers of children and were given money to support those large families. They relied on that stipend and had more children, or they relied on the promise of retirement money and retired. In a year, the things they were encouraged not to think about became all-important, and most of the things they had taken for granted were gone. They had skills that were sometimes worth nothing, children they could not afford to support, and money that was worth less all the time. From these desperate circumstances, for some, social problems have arisen that Mongolians before had been spared.

ALCOHOLISM

Although Mongolians have always enjoyed vast amounts of the mildly alcoholic *airag*, the country's serious problems with alcoholism began with the introduction of Soviet vodka during the Communist era. The government built its first vodka distillery in Mongolia in 1959 and launched an advertising campaign on behalf of alcohol consumption. Members of the Mongolian Youth League traveled the country promoting modest consumption. The advertising campaign worked a little too well. Mongolians' genetics are responsible for the effect of alcohol upon them. They lack a blood enzyme that breaks down alcohol and so are prone to becoming drunk easily.

The problem has worsened since the transition to democracy. Widespread unemployment, poverty, and confusion about their role in society have driven people to drink. Officers of the Ministry of Health call the situation a "crisis"; 51 percent of adult Mongolians are thought to "drink excessively." The average urban Mongolian drinks 8.5 gallons of vodka per year. Drunkenness is blamed for 60 percent of all crimes, including 48 percent of all murders. Alcoholism is also estimated to cause 30 percent of divorces.

The government and the private sector have attempted a variety of solutions to the problem. For a while, the police were using the old Russian detoxification trick of injections to make the body reject alcohol. Police have also tried punishment, forcing drunks detained more than four times to go to work on the first true highway linking eastern and western Mongolia. Those who recognize they have a problem on their own have access to a rehabilitation program similar to Alcoholics Anonymous introduced by the American group Joint Christian Services.

DOMESTIC VIOLENCE

Alcohol abuse may in turn fuel violence against spouses and children. Mongolian society has tended not to be open about such issues, either pretending a problem does not exist or considering it something to be dealt with inside the family. Information on the prevalence of domestic violence is, therefore, limited, but it is thought that up to one-third of the female population is affected by spousal abuse. In 2000, more than 30 percent of people punished by the administrative system had been involved in domestic violence, and half of that 30 percent were charged with spousal abuse. Even these figures are believed to underestimate the problem, as many women will not prosecute for fear of losing the income of a partner.

STREET CHILDREN

Perhaps even more disturbing, family violence is believed to be a major cause of children leaving home and living on the street, often in sewers.

Estimates of the number of street children living in the cities in Mongolia range from 2,000 to 4,000. Many of these are only on the streets some of the time, say the daytime or in the summer, to make money to take back to their families. Observers estimate that about 400 children actually live in the streets full time.

Most of the street children come to the streets at about age 10 or 12. As well as fleeing domestic violence, they come because they have been abandoned by parents or other caregivers or there is not enough food at home. On the street, they try to earn a little money by hanging around markets and offering to clean up garbage, make deliveries, etc. They get food either by buying it with the little money they earn, looking in rubbish bins, begging at shops or restaurants, or stealing. A butcher might give the children a bone, for example. The children will scrape off the meat with their fingernails and cook it into a soup. When children steal and are caught, they sometimes just get a warning from the police. If they are older and more threatening, they may get sent to a children's prison on a charge for breaking and entering, for example.

The street children's health is poor. The very cold Mongolian winters are particularly hard on them. Children form groups to stay warm, and they sleep either in apartment building stairways, luggage racks on trains, or underground. The most common place for them to sleep is the spaces over underground hot-water pipes. When these burst, as sometimes happens, the children are scalded. Because they do not have access to washrooms to clean themselves, the children are also vulnerable to skin diseases. Sexually transmitted diseases are also extremely common, as many of the girls turn to prostitution to earn money.

HEALTH

Poor health does not only afflict the street children. Increased poverty, increased problems with infrastructure, and a decline in organization and availability of the health care system have resulted in poorer health for the entire population since the transition to democracy. Health care under the Communists was free and emphasized prevention. Health care is no longer free and provided by the government, and so people are not likely to seek it out until illnesses are serious. Poverty, and the consequent lack of food, also increase malnutrition. It is estimated that 37 percent of

Mongolian children have rickets, a problem caused by vitamin D deficiency.

Many of the country's health problems also relate to traditional practices that have always been unhealthy but have yet to be eradicated. For example, almost all Mongolian *ger* are heated with dung, wood, or coal, with only minimal air exchange with the outside. This is believed to contribute to high rates of respiratory infection among Mongolian children. Even the nomadic lifestyle has its perils. One mother's infant became ill with pneumonia when left outside on a cart while the family constructed its *ger* at a new camp. It was a cold and rainy spring day, and since the *ger* had not yet been built, there was no shelter. Pneumonia is the leading cause of infant mortality in Mongolia.

Other illnesses come as a result of Mongolians' close interactions with animals. The dogs that guard *ger* and herds may acquire rabies and pass it on to humans. For the last decade, the plague (the Black Death that decimated Europe in the Middle Ages) has appeared in Mongolia every summer after the ban on hunting marmots ceases. Marmots—small furry rodents—carry the plague. Mongolians hunt them for food and fur. When they hang them up to skin them, blood can fly into the hunter's face, causing infection. Sharing water with animals, as Mongolians do, also passes infections.

The Mongolian health system even at its best is ill-equipped to deal with these problems. Distances are vast, and communication and transportation in the event of an emergency in the countryside are difficult. Even in cities, hospitals do not have their own electricity generators, as hospitals in the West do. Because its energy system is poor, Mongolia has frequent blackouts. Every year, people die in the midst of routine operations when the power goes out in the hospital they are being treated in. Mongolia does not appear to have a large problem with HIV/AIDS, but in any case it cannot afford to screen donated blood for the virus, so it is possible it is transmitted through transfusions. Only a few dozen physicians staff Ulaanbaatar's emergency number (103), and it can take 25 minutes for an ambulance to arrive, even in the city.

In an effort to fill the gaps left by modern medicine, Mongolians have revived traditional medicine, which was suppressed by the Communists. A wolf's intestines are supposedly good for an upset stomach. A woodchuck's gallbladder is thought to cure toothache. Marmot oil is used to treat burns, and it is believed that eating the left kidney of a marmot raw will heal a human's left kidney. Human urine is also a traditional medicine in Mongolia. The Institute of Traditional Medicine in Ulaanbaatar is trying to determine which of these and other techniques are effective, and which are counterproductive. Less controversially, the institute sponsors acupuncture, massage, and mineral water and mud bath treatments. International organizations are also trying to help. The World Health Organization, for example, has begun a Reproductive Health Project in Mongolia. It recently donated a German-made medical diagnostic apparatus and had instruction manuals for it translated into Mongolian. The apparatus allows Mongolian doctors to detect anemia, an illness caused by iron deficiency, which is the main cause of women dying during pregnancy in Mongolia.

NOTES

p. 98 "'Abandon negative action . . .'" Thubten Chodron, *Buddhism for Beginners* (Ithaca, N.Y.: Snow Lion Publications, 2001), p. 13.

p. 100 "The path to Nirvana . . ." Chodron, *Buddhism for Beginners*, p. 13.

p. 100 "Other Buddhas include . . ." Mayhew, *Mongolia*, pp. 44–45.

p. 100 "For example, the historical . . ." Mayhew, *Mongolia*, p. 44.

pp. 100–101 "Representations of the Buddha . . ." Chodron, Buddhism for Beginners, pp. 22–23.

p. 101 "Tara, the Savior . . ." Mayhew, *Mongolia*, p. 45.

p. 101 "Shamanism has as its goal . . ." Golomt Center for Shamanist Studies, "A Course in Mongolian Shamanism—Introduction 101," on Shaman South website. Available on-line. URL: http://www.geocities.com/RainForest/ Vines/2146/mongolia/cms.htm. Updated October 3, 1997.

p. 102 "Mongolians believe . . ." Mayhew, *Mongolia*, p. 47.

p. 102 "This process subjects . . ." U.S. Department of State, Bureau of Democracy, Human Rights and Labor, "Country Reports on Human Rights Practices: Mongolia," March 4, 2002. Available on-line. URL: http://www.state.gov/g/drl/rls/ hrrpt/2001/eap/8357.htm. Posted March 4, 2002.

p. 103 "According to storytellers . . ." N. Enkhbayar, "Practiced Sporting Games Add to Survival Skills," in *Ger Magazine*, Issue 3, January, 2000. Available on-line. URL: http://www.un-mongolia.mn/archives/germag/.

p. 104 "'Because of a foolish owner . . .'" Quoted in "Ghi-i-i-ngho-o! Call of Victory," in *Mongolia Today*, Issue 4. Available on-line. URL: http:// www.mongoliatoday.com/issue/4/horse_race.html. Posted 1999–2002.

p. 104 "'Eye-pleasing . . .'" Mayhew, *Mongolia*, p. 161.

p. 105 "'supermarket of tricks . . .'" Quoted in "'Supermarket' of Wrestling Tricks," in *Mongolia Today*, Issue 3. Available on-line. URL: http://www.mongoliatoday. com/issue/3/supermarket_tricks.html. Posted 1999–2002.

p. 107 "'Ah yes, Michael Jordan . . .'" Michael Kohn, "There Is Nowhere to Half Pipe, But You Can Still Kick Some Air on Sukhbaatar Square," in *Ger Magazine*, Issue 1, September 9, 1998. Available on-line. URL: http://www.un-mongolia.mn/archives/ger-mag/.

p. 107 "'On that day . . .'" Consulate of Mongolia, "Tradition and Customs." http://www.mongolia.org.hk/country_info-6-01.htm.

p. 108 "'Don't call a man . . .'" T. Enkhbold, "Tsagaan Sar, the Lunar New Year," in *Mongolia Today*, Issue 2. Available on-line. URL: http://www.mongoliatoday.com/issue/2/tsagaan_sar_1.html. Posted 1999–2002.

p. 108 "President Bagabandi . . ." BBC News, "Mongolia Glorifies Genghis Khan," May 3, 2002. Available on-line. URL: http://news.bbc.co.uk/1/hi/world/asia-pacific/1967201.stm.

p. 109 "'It was different . . .'" Quoted in Ts. Mongontsetseg and A. Delgermaa, "Marriage—Mongolian Style," in *Ger Magazine*, Issue 3, January, 2000. Available on-line. URL: http://www.unmongolia.mn/archives/ger-mag/.

p. 109 "In 1999, 98 . . ." Mongontsetseg and Delgermaa, *Ger Magazine*, Issue 3.

p. 109 "'I asked my girlfriend . . .'" Mongontsetseg and Delgermaa, *Ger Magazine*, Issue 3.

p. 110 "The average age . . ." Mongontsetseg and Delgermaa, *Ger Magazine*, Issue 3.

p. 110 "'Happy is he . . .'" Quoted in Marlene Targ Brill, Mongolia (Chicago: Children's Press, 1992), p. 94.

p. 110 "Older or esteemed guests . . ." Consulate of Mongolia, "Traditions and Customs," http://www.mongolia.org.hk/country_info-6-01.htm.

p. 111 "A Westerner . . ." Mayhew, *Mongolia*, p. 87.

p. 111 "'Shifting emotions . . .'" Quoted in L. Badamkhand, "Understanding Mongols," in *Mongolia Today*, Issue 4. Available on-line. URL: http://www.mongoliatoday.com/issue/4/mentality.html. Posted 1999–2002.

p. 111 "'I think American . . .'" Michael Kohn, "There Is Nowhere to Half Pipe, But You Can Still Kick Some Air on Sukhbaatar Square," in *Ger Magazine*, Issue 1, September 9, 1998. Available on-line. URL: http://www.unmongolia.mn/archives/ger-mag/.

p. 113 "As of 2000 . . ." "Welcome to *Ger Magazine*!," in *Ger Magazine*, Issue 4, May, 2000. Available on-line. URL: http://www.unmongolia.mn/archives/ger-mag/.

p. 113 "Due to a lack . . ." Jill Lawless, "Money May Be Tight, but Mongolians Are Still Going Online, Booting Up, and Sending Emails," in *Ger Magazine*, Issue 2, May 12, 1999. Available on-line. URL: http://www.unmongolia.mn/archives/ger-mag/.

p. 114 "As of 1999 . . ." *Ger Magazine*, Issue 2.

p. 115 "Many people complain . . ." U.S. Dept. of State—Bureau of Democracy, Human Rights and Labor, "Country Reports on Human Rights Practices: Mongolia," March 4, 2002. Available on-line. URL:http://www.state.gov/ g/drl/rls/hrrpt/2001/eap/8357.htm. Posted March 4, 2002.

p. 116 "Students can reportedly . . ." Mayhew, *Mongolia*, pp. 34–35.

p. 117 "Mongolians' genetics . . ." L. Badamkhand, "Understanding Mongols," in *Mongolia Today*, Issue 4. Available on-line. URL: http://www.mongoliatoday. com/issue/4/mentality.html. Posted 1999–2002.

p. 117 "Drunkenness is blamed . . ." Apples for Health, "Weaning Mongolia off the Bottle," June 28, 2002. Available on-line. URL: http://www. applesforhealth.com/GlobalHealth/wmotbot4.html.

p. 117 "In 2000 . . ." U.S. Dept. of State—Bureau of Democracy, Human Rights and Labor, "Country Reports on Human Rights Practices: Mongolia," March 4, 2002. Available on-line. URL: http://www.state.gov/g/drl/rls/hrrpt/2001/eap/ 8357.htm. Posted March 4, 2002.

p. 117 "Even these figures . . ." U.S. Dept. of State—Bureau of Democracy, Human Rights and Labor, "Country Reports on Human Rights Practices: Mongolia," March 4, 2002. Available on-line. URL: http://www.state.gov/g/drl/rls/ hrrpt/2001/eap/8357.htm. Posted March 4, 2002.

p. 118 "Because they do not have access . . ." Street Children Section, "Have Your Say." Available on-line. http://mongolia.worldvision.org.nz/yoursay/ yoursayans.asp?category=2.

pp. 118–119 "It is estimated . . ." Richard Smith, "Turning Mare's Milk Into Antibiotics," in Ger Magazine, Issue 3, January, 2000. Available on-line. URL: http://www.un-mongolia.mn/archives/ger-mag/.

p. 119 "One mother's infant . . ." Smith, *Ger Magazine*, Issue 3.

p. 119 "Only a few dozen . . ." "When in the Capital, Know Who to Call," in *Ger Magazine*, Issue 3, January, 2000. Available on-line. URL: http://www. un-mongolia.mn/archives/ger-mag/.

p. 119 "A wolf's intestines . . ." Pang, *Mongolia*, p. 71.

8

ART

Mongolian art has much in common with Chinese art: the prevalence of Buddhist themes and bright colors, use of silk, jade, and intricate carving. In fact, much of Mongolian "high" art (as opposed to popular arts or crafts) is Buddhist in inspiration, and Mongolia has historically imported silk and stones from China. But Mongolian art is also heavily influenced in its shape, size, and aesthetic (nature of beauty) by the nomadic culture in which it grew up. With the exception of objects designed for monasteries, which have fixed locations, art, like everything else, had to be small and transportable. This has meant that Mongolian art has largely consisted of useful objects made more beautiful than they need to be through ornamentation, coloration, carving, bejeweling, and so forth. Art has also varied by region, since Mongolian society was so decentralized for most of its history. Thus, the Borjigin clan is known for jewelry, the Dariganga for silverware, the Dalaivang for ironwork, the Oirad for leatherwork, and the Hanhui and Uyanga for painting and carving of wood. The Gobi and Irjin are known for *hoshmog* (colored ribbons for women's clothes). The craftspeople of Ulaanbaatar are known for miniature bronze sculptures, musical instruments, and appliqué work.

With the fall of communism, Buddhist art hidden in caves or abroad has been brought back into public display; new religious art is being created. Traditional music and dances flourish, some having been suppressed and some not. In addition, Mongolia has warmly embraced Western

The herding animals play a large role even in Mongolian art. This wood carving was created by Master Gebschi of the Ulaanbaatar fellowship of artists. (Courtesy Library of Congress)

influences, combining them with traditional modes to create modern Mongolian art. We survey Mongolian art by type.

Clothing

The traditional Mongolian article of clothing, for both men and women, is the *del*. Made of wool, leather, or silk, it is a long robe-like garment with a stand-up collar and fastenings at the throat and across to one side. *Dels* are often embroidered and usually brightly colored. The choice of decoration may indicate the ethnic identity of the wearer. Mongolians usually have more than one *del*, for different seasons and occasions. Winter *del* may be lined with sheepskin, red fox fur, wolf fur, or lambswool for warmth. Though worn in the cities as well as the countryside, the *del* is ideally designed for nomadic life. It has slits down both sides to make horseback riding in it easier and to help pad the rider during long journeys. It may serve as a tent in bad weather or provide an extra blanket. The shape also allows women to go to the bathroom without revealing much.

The *del* is fastened with a long, thin sash (usually silken) tied around the waist. Because a *del* has no pockets, Mongolians will tie objects to the sash to keep them handy. Such objects include eating utensils (knife, chopsticks, possibly toothpick), tweezers, tobacco and pipe pouches, a snuff bottle, and a tinder pouch for starting a fire. These useful, everyday objects may be highly decorated. Chopsticks may be made of ivory with silver tips. Snuff boxes may be made of precious materials like chalcedony (a quartz-like rock), jade, jasper, agate, turquoise, silver, rock crystal, topaz, porcelain, and ebony or another rare wood (wood in general is somewhat rare in Mongolia). The pipe may have a mouthpiece of jade or chry-solite, with a bowl of intricately worked metal. Pipes and the snuff boxes are both often carried in embroidered silk pouches.

Underneath the *del*, Mongolians wear heavy pants tucked into boots.

The traditional Mongolian clothing for men and women: del, *boots, and hat.* (Courtesy Library of Congress)

The traditional boots are made of felt or leather. They look a bit elfin, with pointed, upturned toes. To Mongolians, this shape has religious significance. The shape causes less of the boot to touch the ground, which in turn lessens the trampling of things underfoot, like bugs. This is in keeping with Buddhist beliefs about the sanctity of all life. The open space in the toes also creates a pocket of warm air that provides comfort in the winter.

There are many styles of hats (also necessary in the winter). One popular cold-weather style is the *loovuus*. It is made of fox fur but has a cloth top and an open back. Fox fur is so dense and warm that Mongolians believe that garments made from it without an open back would cause high blood pressure and headaches. (Because of the climate they live in, Mongolians are far more accustomed to cold weather than other people are.) There is also an elaborate traditional headdress for women called the *ugalz*. Meaning "sheep-horn headdress," the *ugalz* indeed resembles the twisted horns on either side of a mountain sheep's head. Mongolian noblewomen's hair would be shaped and hardened using congealed mutton fat and adorned with silver and turquoise beadwork, tassels, and amulets (charms). In such a style, the hair might stick out some 10 inches on either side of the head.

Mongolians also made elaborate saddles, some of brocaded silk with tassels, some with striped or stamped Tibetan wool, many with intricate leather appliqué work or silver beading and ornaments.

Visual Art for Display

Mongolians have also produced more conventional forms of art—sculptures and paintings. The subject of both kinds of art was usually religious. Mongolian sculptors, of which the most famous was Zanabazar (1635–1723), carved images of the various Buddhist gods from bronze or copper-like metals. In many cases, religious texts dictated the proportions of each god, but details were at the discretion of the artist. Zanabazar's school of sculpture often gilded with mercury, a highly toxic metal, or "cold gold" (gold powder mixed with yak-skin glue to make a paint) the faces of the deities it rendered. Using other mineral pigments, the hair of calm gods would be painted blue, and that of angry gods red or orange.

Bronze incense pan by Mongolian sculptor Zanabazar. (Courtesy Library of Congress)

Mongolians also made *thangkas*, or religious scroll paintings. First, the painter would stretch cotton cloth on a frame. Then, the cotton would be treated with a mixture of chalk, glue, and milk vodka. Once it dried, polish would be applied to the surface with a stone. The artist would then draft the image with charcoal, filling in colors by mixing yak-skin glue with mineral or vegetable colors. Common themes were the five principal Mongolian animals (camels, horses, yaks, sheep, and goats), mountains, and clouds. Such paintings could also be incredibly intricate, multi-scene works depicting, for example, significant moments in the conversion of Mongolia to Buddhism. *Thangkas* were often used as aids in Buddhist meditation.

Book decoration was also a religious art in Mongolia (most books prior to the 20th century in Mongolia were religious texts). This was apparent both in the printing of the text itself and in the decoration of the cover. Lamaseries (monasteries) might produce real gold printing on pages of sandalwood paper, for example. Other important texts were printed in gold on black paper. Some texts were actually embossed on sheets of silver or gold. A sacred 10-volume Sanduijud (a Buddhist sutra, or scripture), for example, is made of 110 pounds of gold and silver. To produce more color, monks sometimes ground up each of the "nine jewels" (gold, silver, coral, pearls, lapis lazuli, turquoise, steel, copper, and mother-of-pearl) for use as pigments. Covers were often brocaded silk framed in wood.

Among more modern, secular painters, Balduugiyn Sharav (1869–1939) is well known. Born in 1869 in a monastery, he traveled throughout Mongolia observing and painting daily life. *One Day in the Life of Mongolia*, his most famous work, depicts a variety of activities in the national life.

Music

In a mobile, nomadic society, music and dance were important, easily transportable forms of art. Singing plays a functional role in the herding society, as well as providing entertainment. There are songs to call stray animals back to the herd, songs to direct a horse where to move, songs for making camp and to praise the land, and songs to coax female animals to nurse their babies. Within this last category, there are songs specially suited to the temperament of each type of animal.

Sheep, for example, are known as caring mothers that sometimes need a little pampering or encouragement. Herders sing the following song while caressing the breast of the sheep, sometimes for hours:

> The spring weather comes
> The spring storm starts
> You will feel cold from your side
> Who will you shelter on your side?

Camels, on the other hand, are considered kind animals that nevertheless neglect their offspring. Herdspeople believe that camels are very connected and sympathetic to people, however, and will pay attention and obey people when sung to. Male herders, therefore, sing the camel the Hoosloh song accompanied by the horsehead fiddle (see below).

> Why aren't you accepting
> The sweet little baby

Come to you to have
Your creamy milk
Huus huus huus
huus, huus, huus

Why are you leaving
Your little baby alone and orphan
Who come to you
To grow up, having your milk
The little baby runs in the evening around you
Feed, please with your warm milk
Huus, huus, huus,
huus, huus, huus.

If many singings of this song do not persuade the mother to nurse its baby, the herder will sing the song to a different female camel to try to persuade it to adopt the baby.

Other Mongolian songs are traditionally divided into two categories, short and long songs. Short songs deal with routine everyday activities, nature, and love. Long songs are more serious and philosophical, formal in structure, and act as a form of literature. The original long songs date back some 800 years and were written for weddings, festivals, and religious ceremonies. Long songs can further be divided into three categories, "lesser long songs," "long songs," and "majestic long songs." Some long songs have as many as 20,000 lines and are sung only by special performers. Schools throughout Mongolia teach the technique. The current "long song diva" of Mongolia is Norovbanzad. Major concerts are staged every year in Ulaanbaatar.

Mongolians, like Tibetans, have another very difficult, specialized style of singing called throat-singing, split-tone singing, or *hoomi*. If you have never heard *hoomi* (some groups of Tibetan monks travel the United States demonstrating it), it is difficult to imagine the sound. When you do hear it, it is difficult to believe that only one person can produce the sound. Traditionally, it was performed only by men, because it requires very strong abdominal and throat muscles. It requires the singer to "sing" a growl-like bass note with the abdomen while at the same time singing a whistling, high-pitched tune with the throat and nose. To hear an example of *hoomi*, visit N. Enkhbayar,

Mongolian master throat singer Kongar-ol Ondar has performed with such artists as Grateful Dead drummer Mickey Hart, Frank Zappa, the Kronos Quartet, and Ry Cooder. (AP/Wide World Photos/Mickey Krakowski)

"Mongolian Throat Singing: A National Art Treasure" in Issue 4 of *Ger Magazine*, http://www.un-mongolia. mn/archives/ger-mag/ or check out *Genghis Blues*, a film on the subject.

Musical instruments often accompany singing, or are used on their own. Folk instruments can be broken down either by the material they are made of or by the way that they create music. Mongolian folk instruments may be made of metal, bamboo, other woods, stone, or clay. There are also wind instruments, the *bishguur*, *limbe* (flute-like), *buree*; stringed instruments, the *khuur*, *khuuchir*, *biwa*, *tobshuur* (a swan-necked lute), and python-skin; and various drums. The classic quintet for performances consists of the *shudraga*, a three-stringed lute with a circular sound-box made of wood and covered with skin; the *khuuchir*, a two-stringed spiked fiddle covered in skin; the *yoching*, a board zither; the *limbe*; and the *morin khuur*.

Of all of these, the best loved is the *morin khuur*, the horsehead fiddle. It is made of wood with a carved horse's head at its top. The bow and string are made of hair from a horse's tail. According to tradition, the instrument was originally made as a testament to a rider's dead horse. The animal's rib bones and mane were used to make an instrument capable of expressing grief over the animal's death. Roving entertainers traditionally

This horsehead fiddle, or morin khuur, *the most popular Mongolian instrument, was made by Master Abirmid of Ara-Changaj.* (Courtesy Library of Congress)

used the horsehead fiddle to accompany themselves in performances in exchange for food and lodging. The horsehead fiddle is also used to coax camels into nursing. Mongolians believe the sweet sound makes the camels cry and their milk flow.

In addition to these, some unusual instruments are used for particular religious purposes. A shell-shaped bugle called a *dun* is used to call lamas to ceremonies. A Ganlin horn, made of the femur (upper leg bone) of an 18-year-old female virgin who died of natural causes, is used to dispel bad spirits. Although there is nothing inhumane in the making of this instrument, it is somewhat controversial.

Popular/Modern Music

Since the transition to democracy, Mongolia has experienced an explosion in the popularity and availability of rock music. MTV is available on cable, and bootleg compact discs circulate widely. Hurd (Speed) was one of the first rock groups to form in Mongolia and remains popular. Hurd is a heavy-metal band, citing Metallica and AC/DC as major influences, but its soft ballads are played more often on Ulaanbaatar's radio stations. These include "Girl in a Painting" and "Don't Cry." Unlike a Western band's, Hurd's lyrics tend to be about the group members' parents and the mother country. "We worship our parents. If it wasn't for them, we would not be here," says Otgonbayar, a member of Hurd. "If we translated our lyrics, people elsewhere (could) listen to the words, and they would love their parents more." Otgonbayar taught himself to play the drums by practicing on cups in the countryside.

Other artists and groups are pushing the boundaries of previously conservative Mongolia. Pop singer T. Ariunaa, for example, is known as the Madonna of Mongolia. She is known not so much for the quality of her voice as for her enjoyment of scanty clothing. She often dances and sings in a black silk robe over black underwear. Har Sarnai (Black Rose), a hip-hop/techno male duo, is outrageous in other ways. They like to take the stage wearing specially designed silk *del*, sunglasses, and large bushy black-and-gray wigs. They also do synchronized dancing similar to that of American boy bands.

Many of the artists, including Har Sarnai, believe that they are doing more than making music. They feel a responsibility to create a sound that is modern and fast, but also authentically Mongolian. Har Sarnai tends to have nationalistic lyrics. Hurd leader D. Ganbayar says, "The Mongolian people, and especially the youth, don't want [their bands] to imitate western rock art. They want a pop-rock with its own specific character. . . . We serve our people. It's our duty to introduce western music to the Mongolian people through the Mongolian language and Mongolian melodies."

Dance

Mongolians share with the Chinese and many other societies the tradition of masked dances, known in Mongolia as *tsam*. Because the Communists suppressed them, they are now very seldom held. The *tsam* is a spiritual dance, designed to exorcise evil spirits. *Tsam* has been part of Mongolian tradition since the eighth century and flourished in the Buddhist era inaugurated in Mongolia by Altan Khan. Hundreds of monasteries had their own individual masks and dances. The masks are usually made of papier-mâché and clay and adorned with tassels, horsehair, precious stones, leather, silk, gilt, and glass eyes. As with the sculptures of the Buddhist gods described above, some of the *tsam* masks are friendly and some are fearsome. One common masked character, the white old man, symbolizes the end of one year and the fresh beginning of a new one. In his dance, he initially appears feeble, then gains energy. Citipati, lord of the funeral pyre, is depicted with a huge skull-mask with three empty eye sockets. He wears a crown of five other jeweled skulls and rainbow-colored fans. Garuda, a half-vulture, half-man, is one of the Lords of the Four Mountains. He is depicted with an orange face, gilt eyebrows, a jeweled crown and a cotton snake hanging out of his mouth.

Modern Dancing/Night Life

Dancing and night life have exploded—mostly in Ulaanbaatar—since the democratic revolution. Whereas under communism the only nightspot was government-run, now there are some 600 bars and discos in a city of about 600,000. Many are located in former government buildings but feature Western touches. Club Manhattan, for example, has a huge U.S. flag covering the ceiling and a Statue of Liberty coming out of the wall. When Manhattan opened, it turned on the first high-powered floodlight ever in the country, sweeping across the sky to announce the club's presence. The next day, the main Mongolian newspaper reported that an alien spacecraft had landed in downtown Ulaanbaatar.

Western influences also blend with tradition in other ways at Mongolian nightspots. While Mongolians are eager to learn Western dance moves, they were trained in ballroom dancing under communism and often revert to a fast-paced version of it. In Top Ten, a large club, teenage girls celebrate Mongolian heritage with Genghis Khan beer while sporting Western fashions. The bar at the expensive Khan Brau brew-pub is modeled on a *ger* but is patronized in large part by Westerners. "We can't afford to come here often, but it's nice once in a while," said a Mongolian woman in her twenties. Indeed, the bill for a long night at the pub can easily exceed a Mongolian's monthly paycheck.

Literature

Once again, Mongolia's literature is a reflection of its nomadic society. Until the 20th century, much of it, was oral. Like the Greeks and, closer by, the Hindus of India, Mongolians have a great epic tradition. Even more so than the long songs discussed on page 129, epics are immensely long works—sometimes hundreds of thousands of verses—that require great concentration and memory to recite and were handed down in various forms throughout Russia, Mongolia, and China. The "triple masterpieces" of the Mongolian epic tradition are the *Geser*, the *Jangar*, and the *Secret History of the Mongols*.

In *Geser*, Heaven (Tenger) sends the main hero, Geser, to Earth to rid it of disturbances and impurities. Like the heroes of epics the world over, Geser experiences untold difficulties on his mission, overcoming all of them. His enemies include khans, or princes, bad lamas, and *mangas* (many-headed monsters). Tenger aids Geser when he absolutely needs it, but in general Geser relies on his 33 heroic friends. These include the clever and gutsy Tsaschiher, the wise Buidan, and the smart queen Azu Mergen. In one of its unabridged versions, *Geser* is 100 volumes long.

Jangar is concerned more with ordinary life, although its heroes possess supernatural powers. It concerns life in the land of Tansag Bumba and offers images corresponding to a herding Mongolian's vision of paradise: heavenly grasslands, eternal summer, youth, and immortality. It is divided into 26 chapters that can each stand independently as a story. Like *Geser*, its original author is unknown and, in a way, immaterial, as thousands of retellings have no doubt added to and changed the epic. It is thought that it was probably first created in the 12th or 13th centuries, but it was not actually written down or published until modern times.

Unlike *Geser* and *Jangar*, the *Secret History of the Mongols* was actually written down either at the time of its creation, thought to be around 1240, or not long afterward. It represents a mythologizing of actual people and events in Mongolian history: Genghis Khan, his ancestors and descendants, and their conquests. It was designed to be secret not from the Mongolians but from the Chinese. Mongolians feared that the story might earn them a reputation for barbarism, although the concern was a little belated.

It tells the story of Genghis's upbringing in great detail, including many poetic speeches with vivid nature imagery. Nature is a source of wisdom for Mongolians. For instance, after Genghis and his brother kill their older brother for stealing food, their mother rebukes them:

The one of you . . . was born clasping a black blood-clot in his hand. The other was like the wild dog that devours its own afterbirth. You are like the panther that dashes itself against the cliffside, like the lion that cannot quell its wrath, like the boa-constrictor that swallows its prey alive, like the falcon that flings itself at its own shadow, like the pike that gulps silently, like the randy he-camel that bites the heels of its own young, like the wolf that works havoc under cover of the snow-storm, like the mandarin-duck that eats the ducklings that cannot keep pace with her . . . With no friend but your own shadow, no whip but your own tail, having suffered at the hands of the Taichi'uts such wrongs as cannot be endured, how are you going to take vengeance? I was just wondering how you would get through, and now you must needs do a thing like this?

The speech is powerful but also ambiguous, especially in a text that glorifies Genghis Khan. Is Genghis's mother criticizing all violence or only violence that hurts one's own cause? The speech demonstrates that *The Secret History* is willing to give critics of Genghis their say, and it presents a somewhat balanced portrayal of the man and his development.

Mongolia also has a tradition of vivid folktales, mostly about the animals with whom Mongolians spend so much time. In these tales, four "strong" or good animals figure prominently: the lion, the dragon, the elephant, and the Garuda, the mythical half-bird, half-man described above in the discussion of masks. Snakes and hedgehogs are usually up to no good. The horse is usually the hero of the story, often possessing magical qualities, such as the ability to fly, predict future events, and give the rider wise counsel.

One folktale attempts to explain both the camel's ugliness and its habit of looking around suspiciously in between drinks of water. In the tale, the camel originally possesses antlers and a long, fluffy tail, while the deer has a bare head and the horse has a wispy tail. Envious, the deer asks to borrow the antlers for a day, promising to return them the next day at the water's edge. The horse, emboldened, then asks to borrow the camel's tail for the same period of time. The camel generously agrees, but when it arrives at the water's edge the next day at the appointed time, it is sorely disappointed, but it keeps looking around in hopes of getting back its beautiful attributes.

Another folktale explains why the bat lives in caves and is nocturnal. It also shows traditional Mongolians' belief that choosing a side and remaining loyal to it even when it comes to war is a good thing. In the tale, the birds and the beasts are fighting an all-out war. Because the bat looks like a bird and a beast, it is able to claim allegiance to whichever side is winning at the time. In the end, the birds and beasts agree to make peace, but neither side accepts the bat, since it failed to be loyal when it counted. Embarrassed and outcast, the bat takes to the caves, where it will not be seen.

Mongolians are also known for their sayings, which are short and easy to pass on. Sometimes these bits of wisdom are put in the form of a triad, or three-line poem. Some examples of triads are:

Three endless
Skies are endless
Wisdom is endless
Stupidity is endless

Three dark
Dark is a person without education
Dark is moonless night
Dark is the house without herd

Three red
Red is sunset on a cold winter day
Red are cheeks of a happy queen
Red are sukhai flowers in a valley

Mongolia's best-known modern poet and playwright is Dashdorjiin Natsagdorj. Born in 1906, he wrote nationalist poems, including *The Four*

Seasons of the Year and *Native Land*, which many Mongolians still know by heart. His short stories "Beauty of the Steppe," "The Winged Dun Horse," "White Month," "Black Tears," and "Tears of a Lama" deal with traditional Mongolian topics. "Star," another famous poem of his, explores the idea of spaceflight well before its time. His plays include *Three Tragic Fates*, the first Mongolian opera. He also was one of the first people to translate foreign literature into Mongolian. Although he went to work for the Communist government and served as secretary for Choibalsan, he evidently was not sufficiently loyal. He was arrested in 1936 and died a year later under mysterious circumstances. Neither his body nor his grave has ever been found. Other writers of his generation were also done to death under communism, including Ayush (1903–38) and Buyannemekh (1902–36).

Where the literature of the independent and early Communist years tended to be about nationalism and Mongolia's glory, themes of labor and the need to change—Communist themes—began to predominate in the published literature of the 1940s, 1950s, and later. *The Rejected Girl* by Ts. Damdinsuren (1928–86), for example, contrasts the dim lot of citizens in pre-revolutionary Mongolia with the social awakening of those living in organized nomad camps under communism. Similar examples include the short stories "How Sol' was Changed," "Three Talk and One Works," and "Teacher and Pupil," all by Damdinsuren.

Art Recovery

Since 1989, Mongolians have been undoing the abuses of the Communist era in a variety of ways. Altangerel, grandson of the monk who buried boxes of Buddhist treasures from a local monastery in desolate caves, went hunting for those boxes in 1990. Having unearthed about half, he rejected large offers from Japanese art dealers and other buyers, saying that he had promised his grandfather to keep the collection together. Altangerel opened a museum in Sainshand, the town nearest the former monastery site, and spends his summers shuttling foreign tourists between Sainshand and the rebuilt monastery. Even now, however, the fate of the artifacts is in jeopardy. There is almost no money for security at the museum. In place of an alarm system, Altangerel and his friends take turns keeping watch. They know that theft of Mongolian Buddhist artifacts, which because of Communist practices are rare and therefore valuable, is a serious problem at Mongolian museums. Stolen art quickly makes its way out of the country and into the hands of foreign art dealers. Altangerel has therefore left half the treasures in the ground, with only he knowing their location. He hopes that increased government funding and tourism will allow him to make improvements, but tourist facilities are still primitive. There is no electricity or running water in the wooden shack tourists stay in while visiting the monastery.

NOTES

p. 126 "To Mongolians, this shape . . ." Mayhew, *Mongolia*, p. 40.

pp. 128–129 "'The spring weather comes . . .'" and "'Why aren't you accepting . . .' " Quoted in Kh. Enkhbatar, "Herder Songs Help Nature to Nurture Newborns," in Ger Magazine, Issue 3, January, 2000. Available on-line. URL: http://www.un-mongolia.mn/archives/ger-mag/.

p. 132 "'We worship . . .'" Quoted in "Hurd: Famous Mongolian Rock Band Aims to Cross Over," in *Ger Magazine*, Issue 4, May, 2000. Available on-line. URL: http://www.un-mongolia.mn/archives/ger-mag/.

p. 132 "'The Mongolian people . . .'" Quoted in Peter Marsh, "Mongolia Sings Its Own Song," in *Ger Magazine*, Issue 1, September 9, 1998. Available on-line. URL: http://www.un-mongolia.mn/archives/ger-mag/.

p. 133 "When Manhattan opened . . ." Michael Kohn, "Uncharted: Ulaanbaatar, Mongolia: Macarena in the Middle of Nowhere," in *Student Traveler Magazine*. Available on-line. URL: http://www.studenttraveler. com/mag/09-99/mongolia.cfm. Site updated September 23, 2002.

p. 133 "'We can't afford . . .'" Michael Kohn, "'Someone Should Build a Place like Disneyland': Are Mongolians Drowning in Bars?," in *Ger Magazine*, Issue 2, May 12, 1999. Available on-line. URL: http://www.un-mongolia.mn/archives/ ger-mag/.

p. 134 "In *Geser* . . ." Consulate of Mongolia, "Oral and Written Literature." Available on-line. URL: http://www.mongolia.org.hk/country_info-5-02.htm. Site updated January 30, 2002.

p. 134 "It is thought . . ." "Jangar: A Historical Masterpiece," in Mongolia: Culture, a culling of Web articles about the country. Available on-line. URL: http://danielroy. tripod.com/cgi-bin/alternate/mongolia/november-2000.html. Posted November, 2000.

p. 134 "It was designed . . ." Arthur Waley, *The Secret History of the Mongols and Other Pieces* (London: George Allen & Unwin Ltd, 1963), p. 7.

p. 135 "'The one of you . . .'" Waley, *The Secret History of the Mongols and Other Pieces*, p. 228.

pp. 135–136 "In the tale, the camel . . ." Pang, *Mongolia*, p. 106.

p. 136 "Another folktale explains . . ." Greenblatt, *Genghis Khan and the Mongol Empire*, pp. 70–72.

p. 136 "'Three endless . . .'" Quoted in "Triad Poems' Paradox," in *Mongolia Today*, Issue 5. Available on-line. URL: http://www.mongoliatoday.com/issue/5/triads.html. Posted 1999–2002.

p. 137 "He was arrested . . ." Consulate of Mongolia, "Oral and Written Literature."

p. 137 "Where the literature . . ." Consulate of Mongolia, "Oral and Written Literature."

p. 137 "Altangerel, grandson . . ." Michael Kohn for *The New York Times*, "Buried Treasure Awaits a Museum," in *The International Herald Tribune*, August 17, 2002. Available on-line. URL: http://www.iht.com/articles/67921.html.

CONCLUSION

The world has only begun getting to know Mongolia, and Mongolia has only begun getting to know the world. Although it has been close to 15 years since the latest stage in the country's long history began, the transition to democracy and a market economy, with all the choices, pitfalls, and opportunities they offer, is incomplete. The government's Action Program for 2000–04 emphasizes economic growth and reform, improvement in living standards, better social services (such as education, transportation, health care), narrowing the gap between rich and poor, and honest government. On the economic front, this program is supposed to include encouragement of economic stability (a difficult task), growing the private sector (as opposed to government-owned enterprises), and making sure all citizens benefit from economic growth. These are all worthy goals, but many of Mongolia's donors question the government's ability and willingness to deliver on them.

Major donors and advisers, such as the Asian Development Bank, have their own economic goals for Mongolia. They would like to see the country build a better safety net, so that when problems like domestic abuse, *dzud*, disability, or border clashes arise, citizens have somewhere to turn. They also emphasize that while Ulaanbaatar has reaped some of the benefits of capitalism, rural areas are left with primitive roads, no communication system, and a lack of the other services that government is better able than individuals to provide. On a more technical level, these organizations emphasize the need for better supervision of banks, to ensure that more do not crash and burn; better laws for dealing with issues between merchants; laws requiring that organizations be more open about their finances so that people can tell whether they are doing well or badly; laws making it easier for foreigners to trade with Mongolia; and increased privatization of companies.

In the midst of all this change, Mongolians must also think about what from the past they wish to preserve. Economic development will threaten their pristine environment if not controlled. Foreign mining companies, hunters, fishermen, and developers in particular have less incentive to protect Mongolia's heritage and resources than Mongolians do. Mongolians need to control their activities while encouraging their investment.

On a day-to-day level, especially as foreign goods flow in and poverty subsides, Mongolians will need to make choices about how they want to live their lives. Do they want to retain their nomadic ways, leaving pastures unfenced and relying on animals for transportation, or do they want to be more modern ranchers, with more machines but perhaps less connection to the land? Do they want to wear Western clothes or the beautiful and functional *del*? Do they want to listen to Western music or preserve their traditions of animal lullabies, long songs, and throat singing? Since the fall of the Mongol Empire, Mongolia has been consistently overwhelmed by outside influences—either Russian or Chinese. Now, will it be overwhelmed by Western or global influences or manage to preserve its unique and beautiful character? The answer depends upon a commitment to honest, representative government and hard thinking about values and priorities. In the face of so many encroaching neighbors, Mongolia has kept its identity for thousands of years. It seems likely that, somehow, it will this time too.

NOTE

pp. 140–141 "Major donors and advisers . . ." Asian Development Bank, "Economic Trends and Prospects in Developing Asia: Mongolia," in Asian Development Outlook 2002. Available on-line. URL: http://www.adb.org/Documents/ Books/ADO/2002/MON.asp. Site updated September 29, 2002.

CHRONOLOGY

500,000 years ago
First physical evidence of human habitation of Mongolia

5000 B.C.
First written evidence (in Chinese dynastic histories) of human habitation of Mongolia

1500 B.C.
Inhabitants of Mongolia switch from farming to herding because of climate change

Third century B.C.
A tribe from Mongolia, the Xiongnu, invade China; the Xiongnu and other Mongolian tribes continue to conquer and be conquered by the Chinese over succeeding centuries

618–907
First use of the word *Mongol,* in the Chinese Tang dynastic histories, to describe the inhabitants of Mongolia

1162
Temujin, the boy who became Genghis (Chinggis) Khan, is born

1206
Temujin acknowledged leader of all the Mongols and named Genghis Khan

1227
Genghis Khan dies

1261–1294

Kublai Khan reigns over Mongolia and China

1400–1454

Two Mongolian tribes, the Oirat and Khalka, fight civil war

1578

Altan Khan converts to Tibetan Buddhism, bringing it to Mongolia

1644–1911

Qing dynasty, based in Manchuria, rules China and Mongolia

1915

China acknowledges independence of Outer (present-day) Mongolia

1917

Russian czar and family overthrown and killed; Russian civil war begins

1919

Mongolia re-surrenders to China

1921

Mongolians repel the Chinese, declare independence

1924

Mongolia becomes a communist state modeled on the Soviet Union

1920s, 1930s

First attempt at collectivization of livestock herds and herding families

1930s

Religious purges at their height

1939–1945

World War II

1952

Joseph Stalin's henchman, Khorloogiyn Choibalsan, dies; the more moderate Yumjaagiyn Tsedenbal succeeds him

1956

Soviets withdraw troops from Mongolia in short-lived period of increased freedoms

1958

Collectivization finally completed

1961

Mongolia joins United Nations

1984

August 23: Tsedenbal replaced by Jambyn Batmonh while visiting the USSR

1985

March: Mikhail Gorbachev rises to power in the Soviet Union

1986

July: USSR begins troop withdrawals, this time for good; glasnost and *shinechal* bring greater freedoms to Soviets and Mongolians, respectively

1989

June: Pro-democracy protesters massacred in Tiananmen Square, Beijing, China

December: Mongolians take to the streets demanding democracy

1990

March: Mongolian revolution ends peacefully, with most of the Communist government resigning

May: Constitution amended to permit multiparty elections

July: First multiparty elections; Communists win in landslide

1991

Family names reinstated; Soviet aid terminated; Mongolian economy forced to stand on its own

1992

Inflation reaches 325 percent; Wild horses reintroduced onto Mongolian steppe

January: Completely overhauled, democratic constitution ratified
June: First election under democratic constitution occurs; again, Communists win in landslide

1993

Democratic candidate P. Ochirbat wins first presidential election under democratic system

1996

First Internet service provider comes to Mongolia

1997

N. Bagabandi, Communist candidate, defeats Ochirbat in presidential election

1998

Winter cycles of *dzud* devastate Mongolian livestock, economy, people
July–October: Constitutional crisis over powers of Khural versus presidency impairs government
October: Revolutionary leader and Democratic politician Sanjaasuren Zorig murdered

2000

July: Communists retake Khural in landslide election

2002

840th anniversary of Genghis Khan's birth publicly celebrated
November: Dalai Lama visits; China warns Mongolian leaders not to meet Tibetan spiritual leader.

FURTHER READING

NONFICTION MATERIALS

Akiner, Shirin, ed. *Mongolia Today*. London and New York: Kegan Paul International, 1991. General look at Mongolian society as of beginning of democratic era.

Andrews, Roy Chapman. *On the Trail of Ancient Man*. New York: G. P. Putnam's Sons, 1926. Tale of the author's dinosaur fossil expeditions in Mongolia and other parts of Central Asia in the 1920s.

Brill, Marlene Targ. *Enchantment of the World: Mongolia*. Chicago: Children's Press, 1992. Young adult book with survey of Mongolian culture and excellent photography.

Chodron, Thubten. *Buddhism for Beginners*. Ithaca, N.Y.: Snow Lion Publications, 2001. Excellent, readable introduction to concepts of Buddhism.

Consulate of Mongolia. "Country Information." Available on-line. URL: http://www.mongolia.org.hk/country_info.htm. Updated on January 30, 2002. Excellent, detailed information on almost all aspects of Mongolian history, culture, and land. The sections on the Communist era seem the least reliable, as the writer seems to have a pro-communist slant.

Greenblatt, Miriam. *Genghis Khan and the Mongol Empire*. New York: Benchmark Books, Marshall Cavendish Corp. 2002.

Griffin, Keith, ed. *Poverty and the Transition to a Market Economy in Mongolia*. London: Macmillan Press Ltd, 1995. Details on economic conditions in Mongolia.

Heissig, Walther. *Religions of Mongolia*. Trans. Geoffrey Samuel. London: Routledge & Kegan Paul, 1980.

Jeffries, Ian. *Economies in Transition: A Guide to China, Cuba, Mongolia, North Korea and Vietnam at the Turn of the 21st Century*. London and New York: Routledge, 2001. Comparison and contrasting of transition experiences of various Communist bloc countries.

Marshall, Robert. *Storm from the East: From Genghis Khan to Khubilai Khan*. Berkeley: University of California Press, 1993. Account of exploits of Mongol conquerors.

Marx, Karl. *Capital: A Critique of Political Economy.* Translated by Ben Fowkes. New York and London: Penguin Books, 1990. Known as *Das Kapital* in the original German, this is the book that first outlined the theory of communism.

Mayhew, Bradley. *Lonely Planet Mongolia* (3d edition). Melbourne, Australia: Lonely Planet Publications Pty Ltd, 2001. Provides information on Mongolian history as well as quirky details about current life there.

Murphy, George S. *Soviet Mongolia: A Study of the Oldest Political Satellite.* Berkeley and Los Angeles: University of California Press, 1966. A detailed study of the first 40 years of communism in Mongolia.

Pang, Guek-Cheng. *Cultures of the World: Mongolia.* New York, London, and Sydney: Marshall Cavendish Corp. 1999. Rich illustrations, survey of Mongolian culture.

Sanders, Alan J. K., "Parliament in Mongolia." Philip Norton and Nizam Ahmed, eds., *Parliaments in Asia.* London and Portland, Oreg.: Frank Cass, 1999. Good discussion of Mongolia's government in the 1990s.

Savada, Andrea Matles, and Robert L. Worden, eds. *Mongolia: A Country Study.* Washington, D.C.: Library of Congress, Federal Research Division, 1991. Nuts-and-bolts guide to Mongolia as of the end of the Communist era.

The Constitution of Mongolia. Available on-line. URL: http://www.indiana.edu/ ~mongsoc/mong/constttn.htm. Downloaded November 9, 2002.

LITERATURE AND ART

Bartholomew, Terese Tse, and Patricia Berger, eds. *Mongolia: The Legacy of Chinggis Khan.* London: Thames and Hudson in Association with Asian Art Museum of San Francisco, 1995. Richly illustrated guide to an exhibition of Mongolian art. Contains essays on a variety of topics in Mongolian culture as well as art.

Damdinsuren, Ts. *Tales of an Old Lama.* Translated by C. R. Bawden. Tring, U.K.: Institute of Buddhist Studies, 1997. Stories by one of Mongolia's most famous modern writers.

Waley, Arthur, trans. *The Secret History of the Mongols and Other Pieces.* London: George Allen & Unwin Ltd, 1963. Contains an abridged translation of *The Secret History.*

INDEX